The Official Story of The Championships

WIMBLEDON
2013

THE CHAMPIONSHIPS WIMBLEDON

MONDAY 24TH JUNE TO SUNDAY 7TH JULY 2013

WIMBLEDON.COM

Designed by Blue Peter competition winner Priya Eardley, aged 8 years.

The Official Story of The Championships

WIMBLEDON
2013

By Neil Harman

(Left) *The official 2013 Championships poster was designed by BBC Blue Peter competition winner Priya Eardley, aged eight years*

VSP

Published in 2013 by Vision Sports Publishing Ltd

Vision Sports Publishing Ltd
19-23 High Street, Kingston upon Thames
Surrey, KT1 1LL
www.visionsp.co.uk

ISBN: 978-1909534-08-7

Written by: Neil Harman
Additional writing by: Alexandra Willis
Edited by: Jim Drewett and Alexandra Willis
Production editor: John Murray
Designed by: Neal Cobourne
Photography: Bob Martin, Tom Lovelock, Matthias Hangst, Dillon Bryden, Jon Buckle, Florian Eisele, David Levenson, Jeff Moore, Chris Raphael and Steve Wake
Picture research: Paul Weaver and Sarah Frandsen

All photographs © AELTC

Results and tables are reproduced courtesy of the AELTC

The All England Lawn Tennis Club (Championships) Limited
Church Road, Wimbledon, London, SW19 5AE, England
Tel: +44 (0)20 8944 1066
Fax: +44 (0)20 8947 8752
www.wimbledon.com

Printed in Slovakia by Neografia

This book is reproduced with the assistance of Rolex.

Contents

Foreword
By Philip Brook
Chairman of The All England Lawn Tennis & Croquet Club and Committee of Management of The Championships

On Friday 3 July 1936, Fred Perry won his third successive Gentlemen's Singles title at Wimbledon, beating Gottfried von Cramm 6-1, 6-1, 6-0 in just 40 minutes of Centre Court action. On the same tennis court, on Sunday 7 July 2013, Andy Murray won his first Wimbledon title, beating Novak Djokovic 6-4, 7-5, 6-4 in three hours and 10 minutes, thereby bringing to an end a wait of 77 years for the next British Wimbledon Gentlemen's Singles champion.

Our congratulations to Andy Murray on his historic win and also to our new Ladies' Singles champion, Marion Bartoli from France, who triumphed over Sabine Lisicki 6-1, 6-4. Our two singles champions collected prize money of £1.6 million for their success in a year when The Championships' overall prize money increased by 40 per cent to over £22.5m.

The 127th Championships will also be remembered for their drama and unpredictable results. By the close of play on the first Thursday, just four days into the Fortnight, seven of the top 16 seeds in the men's singles had been eliminated, including Roger Federer, Rafael Nadal and Jo-Wilfried Tsonga. The ladies' singles proved to be even more perilous, with nine of the top 16 seeds losing in the first two rounds, Victoria Azarenka and Maria Sharapova among them.

The first Wednesday was particularly full of unexpected results, as several players withdrew either before or during a match due to injury. The events of that day reminded us again of the need for a longer period of time between the end of Roland Garros and the start of The Championships to allow players to recover from the French Open and to prepare thoroughly for Wimbledon. We look forward to 2015 and the addition of a third week in the hope that players will be carrying fewer injuries coming into Wimbledon and that they will all take the opportunity to compete on grass as part of their preparation during this important transition period from clay to grass.

The Championships 2013 were also Richard Grier's last as Championships Director after 28 years in the role. We congratulate him on his outstanding contribution and wish him a very happy retirement.

Finally, just a few weeks after The Championships were completed, work began on the Wimbledon Master Plan, our vision for the further improvements to the Grounds at the All England Club which will, inter alia, add a roof to No.1 Court by 2019.

I hope this annual will bring back many happy memories of Wimbledon 2013.

Philip Brook

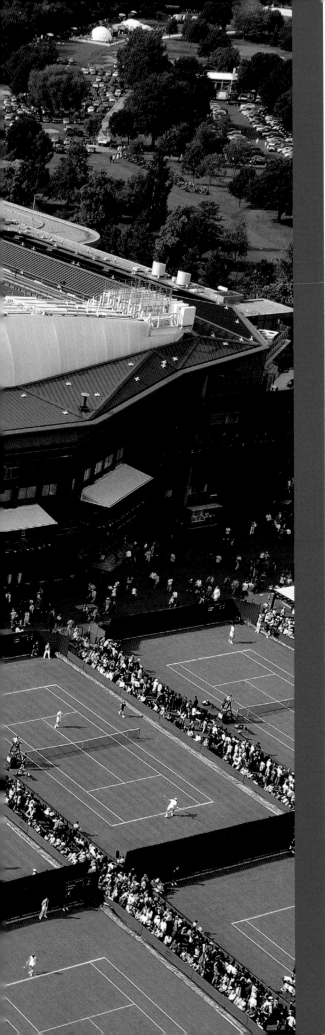

Introduction
By Neil Harman

The Grounds of the All England Club were in their finest fettle a little earlier this year. It was the desire of Philip Brook, the Chairman, and his Committee, that when the players began to arrive for the 127th Championships, there would be more room to move and breathe, less construction work going on and this would add to the sense of anticipation and magic that always fills the air at this time of year.

The workmen were painting the surrounds and varnishing the benches the day I first walked in, five days before the off, to check on the place – there is nothing that quite beats the first view in June from the Centre Court up to St Mary's Church – and see who might be utilising the practice facilities. Suffice to say, Roger Federer was on the Championships courts, on which the leading seeds are allowed to spend an extra hour of preparation in the week before it all gets under way. At 31, and with his sixth Halle title in the bag, Federer radiated health and vitality – much as the environs of the Club.

We had learned in April of the plans for the future prosperity, the Wimbledon Master Plan, including the building of a retractable roof for No.1 Court, which would be completed (or so that was the Club's expectation and they never 'expected' without knowing it would be done) by The Championships 2019. The new roof would guarantee that 25,500 spectators would be able to watch tennis even if it was pelting down outside.

The objectives of the Wimbledon Master Plan are many and all of them in keeping with the prestige of the place. The ambition is that Wimbledon should retain its lofty position in the pantheon of world sporting events while embracing the virtues of 'Tennis in an English Garden', so resonant of its enduring success.

As for 2013, the men's seedings had caused a bit of a stir. Rafael Nadal, fresh (or maybe not so fresh) from his victory at Roland Garros, an incredible eighth victory on the Parisian clay, was the No.5 seed, thus making for a potentially lopsided draw. The initiation of the Club's grass court formula in 2001, ostensibly to prevent players from not participating because they felt the old Committee system conspired against them, had worked well, the small compensation for grass court form mixed into the player's ranking so that sensible dispensation was given to those who succeeded on the surface in its limited timeframe.

Thus, Nadal's loss to Lukas Rosol of the Czech Republic in the second round in 2012, after which he did not play until February 2013 to rest his damaged left knee, counted against him. As luck would have it, Nadal was drawn into the same half as Federer and Andy Murray.

Murray, who had been forced to bypass the French Open to rest his own niggly back injury, rebounded in spectacular fashion to win the Aegon Championships at The Queen's Club. He donated his winner's cheque to the Royal Marsden Hospital, in Sutton, which had been treating his best friend and Great Britain Davis Cup international Ross Hutchins for Hodgkin's lymphoma. It was a stunning gesture.

In Paris, Serena Williams had cemented her position of authority at the top of the women's game and in this year, the 40th anniversary of the birth of the Women's Tennis Association, she was its seminal athlete, bestriding the game at the age of 31 and seemingly invincible.

There would be record prize money on offer for those who were successful – and those not so successful. Wimbledon had announced a 40 per cent improvement in its overall purse, with the champions receiving a 39 per cent increase, to the tune of £1.6 million for the gentleman and lady who prevailed. There really was all to play for.

Wimbledon 2013

Gentlemen's Singles Seeds

Novak Djokovic
(Serbia)
Seeded 1st
Age: 26
Wimbledon titles: 1
Grand Slam titles: 6

Andy Murray
(Great Britain)
Seeded 2nd
Age: 26
Grand Slam titles: 1

Roger Federer
(Switzerland)
Seeded 3rd
Age: 31
Wimbledon titles: 7
Grand Slam titles: 17

David Ferrer
(Spain)
Seeded 4th
Age: 31

Rafael Nadal
(Spain)
Seeded 5th
Age: 27
Wimbledon titles: 2
Grand Slam titles: 12

Jo-Wilfried Tsonga
(France)
Seeded 6th
Age: 28

Tomas Berdych
(Czech Republic)
Seeded 7th
Age: 27

Juan Martin Del Potro
(Argentina)
Seeded 8th
Age: 24
Grand Slam titles: 1

9th Richard Gasquet (France)
10th Marin Cilic (Croatia)
11th Stanislas Wawrinka (Switzerland)
12th Kei Nishikori (Japan)

13th Tommy Haas (Germany)
14th Janko Tipsarevic (Serbia)
15th Nicolas Almagro (Spain)
16th Philipp Kohlschreiber (Germany)

The Seeds

Ladies' Singles Seeds

Serena Williams
(USA)
Seeded 1st
Age: 31
Wimbledon titles: 5
Grand Slam titles: 16

Victoria
Azarenka
(Belarus)
Seeded 2nd
Age: 23
Grand Slam titles: 2

Maria Sharapova
(Russia)
Seeded 3rd
Age: 26
Wimbledon titles: 1
Grand Slam titles: 4

Agnieszka
Radwanska
(Poland)
Seeded 4th
Age: 24

Sara Errani
(Italy)
Seeded 5th
Age: 26

Li Na
(China)
Seeded 6th
Age: 31
Grand Slam titles: 1

Angelique
Kerber
(Germany)
Seeded 7th
Age: 25

Petra Kvitova
(Czech Republic)
Seeded 8th
Age: 23
Wimbledon titles: 1
Grand Slam titles: 1

9th Caroline Wozniacki (Denmark)
10th Maria Kirilenko (Russia)
11th Roberta Vinci (Italy)
12th Ana Ivanovic (Serbia)

13th Nadia Petrova (Russia)
14th Samantha Stosur (Australia)
15th Marion Bartoli (France)
16th Jelena Jankovic (Serbia)

DAY ONE
MONDAY 24 JUNE

The time: 10.30pm; the location: Carluccio's on Wimbledon High Street. The largest occupancy of a single table, set in the middle of the restaurant, was Belgian and the man in the centre of them (as well as being the centre of attention) was Steve Darcis. Time and again, he was asked if he would rise from his chair and pose for a picture as excited patrons realised they were in the company of the 29-year-old from Liège who was the talk of the opening day of The Championships. He willingly acceded to every request, for these are the days to be cherished in the life of any professional athlete.

Rafael Nadal lost in the first round of a Grand Slam for the first time

Well, if Darcis was not exactly *the* talk of the day, he was certainly in second place. Most of the headlines and the images were dominated by Rafael Nadal, who had been beaten in the first round of a Grand Slam tournament for the first time in his career and left the Grounds in a similar state of bemused angst as when he was out-gunned by Lukas Rosol of the Czech Republic in the second round of 2012.

"There is no comparation [Rafa's word for comparison]," he said of his 7-6(4), 7-6(8), 6-4 defeat, and if the styles of Darcis and Rosol could not be more different, the impact of their performances can surely be equally measured. Nadal may have found himself in a robust section of the draw but the absence in number of huge hitters like Rosol around him suggested the left-hander would have time to find his grass court feet, having not played on the surface since he departed Paris with another trophy to chew on.

Then out came Darcis and played in a manner that even he could never have imagined. His previous best results so far in the year had come on the ATP Challenger Tour at less than luxurious venues like Ostrava (he lost in the final to Jiri Vesely of the Czech Republic) and Quimper (he lost in the semi-finals to Marc Giquel of France). The exceptional result he completed with a searing ace down the T against a 12-time Grand Slam champion came distinctly out of the blue. Much of his tennis would not rock an opponent back on his heels, so much that he uses the angles, cuts across the ball with side-spin, moves so beautifully (as all the Belgian players do) and is not intimidated by people with twice his physical force.

Darcis's shot of the match came at 4-3 in the third set when Nadal managed to strike belligerently through a cross-court backhand which ought to have whipped the racket from his opponent's hand, but he strained and half-dived to keep the ball in play. Nadal, tempted forward, netted an attempted drop shot and what might have been 0-30 on the Belgian's serve was 15-15. A break there and who knows what adrenalin rush the Spaniard might have enjoyed? But he did not get it.

So was Nadal at another of his injury crossroads? After his loss to Rosol last year (paradoxically Rosol was in the same queue for a first round loser's cheque after a five-set defeat to German qualifier Julian Reister), the Spaniard was not seen for another seven months, as his knee flared and subsided, along with his levels of confidence. "Can we be optimistic and see you earlier than that this time?" he was asked. "Not very late. Not that late for sure," was the response, as clipped as many of the others he delivered. So could he come back and have a chance of winning again? "I didn't know the answer to that question in 2005, or 2006, or 2007; the only thing I can say is that I will keep working hard and giving myself chances about my game on this surface. I think and hope to have a few more years to play here at the right level. I was not able to play great this year or last year. I'm going to try."

The first-day casualties included the famous and the not so instantly recognised. With his victory over the guardsman-stiff Kenny De Schepper and having tested the full extent of Gilles Simon's talent in Eastbourne, Kyle Edmund was beginning to make a name for himself. Sadly, his first excursion in the Wimbledon first round, courtesy of a wild card, was a straight-sets defeat to Jerzy Janowicz, but this was no mean let-down. The Pole is one of the stars of the future and a horrible pick for the opening round.

As we spoke after his 6-2, 6-2, 6-4 defeat, Edmund was standing across the corridor from a picture of Boris Becker in preparation for one of the serves with which he bludgeoned his way at 17 years of age to the first of three Wimbledon titles. Their hair is the same colour of soft sand, but a look at Becker's legs, the way he carried himself and the lustre of his skills is further evidence of how much this sport has changed in the intervening 28 years.

At 18, Edmund was delighted to be in the field, appreciative of the helping hand that had come his way, and has his eyes fixed firmly on the years ahead and a determination to make good on his skills, which are plentiful. Becker was a rounded champion by that time, his 'Boom-Boom' style echoed across the major courts of the world, and he would not be denied.

Steve Darcis shows his emotion as he celebrates his astonishing upset of Rafael Nadal

Ready? Play ...

As is usual on the first Monday of The Championships, the outside courts were kept busy throughout the day as the bottom half of the men's singles draw and bottom half of the ladies' singles draw all completed their first round matches.

Britain's Kyle Edmund impressed on his Wimbledon main draw debut

Becker must wonder how easily it seemed to come to him and, yes, Edmund probably thought the same. It may well be another six or seven years before the teenager from Beverley fully rounds. Against the 22-year-old Janowicz his early composure was reassuring and yet, once his opponent was into his blistering stride, there was very little he could do to hold him at bay.

Edmund was not alone in feeling the bitter sense of defeat; indeed the first day was littered with casualties. For local consumption, of course, the losses in the ladies' singles for Elena Baltacha, Johanna Konta and Anne Keothavong, and for James Ward in the men's singles, were the toughest to bear. Ward lost in four sets, three of them tie-breaks, to Lu Yen-Hsun of Chinese Taipei, but some starred names disappeared from the scene as well. None was more deeply regretted than the Swiss artist (no, not him) Stanislas Wawrinka, who had been involved in arguably the best Grand Slam match of the year, against Novak Djokovic in the Australian Open in January – over five hours of amazing tennis – and had just returned to the world's top 10. When his name was drawn from the bag to face Lleyton Hewitt, the 2002 champion, something obviously had to give and it was the Swiss, who never quite got into his effective stride – or perhaps that should be that the Australian simply did not let him rest for a minute. Hewitt won 6-4, 7-5, 6-3, a trademark effort from someone who refuses to give in to the thought that the sun will soon have to set on his playing career. His vocabulary does not contain the word 'stop'.

There was almost a shuddering halt to the progress of Victoria Azarenka, the two-time Australian Open champion, and certainly the shriek she emitted after a tumble on No.1 Court against Maria Joao Koehler could have been heard in every corner of the Grounds. It sounded and looked awful but somehow the world No.3 from Belarus was able to continue and defeat the Portuguese 6-1, 6-2. "For two minutes I was in such constant pain, it freaked me out," she said.

Victoria Azarenka was unlucky to suffer an injury during her first round match

With all this going on across the way, Andy Murray's return to Centre Court was decidedly without incident. True, he did play a silly shot when poised for a 5-1 lead in the first set against Benjamin Becker and allowed the German to piece together something of a recovery, but for the most part the world No.2 had the match where he wanted it and secured a 6-4, 6-3, 6-2 victory. He wanted an ordinary day, with not too many alarms, and that is what happened.

While the Belgians were downing a few glasses of champagne on Wimbledon High Street, Murray was sipping still water, quietly contented.

WIMBLEDON IN NUMBERS

135 The ranking of Steve Darcis, the lowest-ranked player to defeat Rafael Nadal in a Grand Slam, and the lowest since world No.690 Joachim Johansson beat the Spaniard in Stockholm in 2006.

A busy first day

The famous Wimbledon Queue was so popular for the first day of The Championships that spectators-to-be were queueing on the pavement even before the Queue opened on Sunday morning! Fans from Great Britain (*above*), Australia (*left*), Switzerland (*below left*) and Belgium (*below*) were among those eager to get inside the gates for one of the most anticipated Championships in recent memory. As is the tradition, visitors to the Grounds were greeted by the Honorary Stewards (*above left*), who were on hand to assist with any questions.

DAY TWO
TUESDAY 25 JUNE

T he days were getting cooler, and stranger. Roger Federer, the bastion of Championships' decorum, was pulled to one side and ticked off for having displayed orange soles on his shoes in the first Centre Court match of The Championships that contravened the Club's 'almost entirely white' clothing policy. He took his chastising with good grace.

Laura Robson celebrated an accomplished first round win against Maria Kirilenko on No.1 Court to rapturous applause

Next we had the sight on Court 18 – where daring deeds have been done and matches have lasted three days before someone had to lose – of Philipp Kohlschreiber, the German 16th seed, retiring in the fifth set against Ivan Dodig of Croatia, offering the novel explanation that he was "totally exhausted" and had no energy left, and the excuse that he hadn't been feeling well.

Then there was the case of poor Guido Pella of Argentina, a left-hander playing his first Grand Slam on grass on Court 7, pulling his adductor muscle with such a force that he had to be carried off on a stretcher and was told by the training staff on site that it would be three weeks before he could pick up a racket. Whether £23,500 as a first round loser was any compensation, we did not know.

Late in the evening, Tara Moore, playing in her first main draw and ranked No.194, was involved in a two-and-a-half hour marathon with Kaia Kanepi, the tall Estonian, before losing 7-5, 5-7, 7-5, but she had shown that she has it in her to mix it with the finer players in the world. This was an encouraging development for the British game which desperately needs decent competitors.

Most enjoyment, however, was to be discovered on No.1 Court, when Laura Robson, in the composed, stylish manner she tends to bring to the biggest of occasions, put the No.10 seed Maria Kirilenko of Russia to flight. Walking away from action at the close of Robson's 6-3, 6-4 victory, I bumped into Judy Murray, the Great Britain Fed Cup captain, who has been privy at close quarters to the developmental progress of the 19-year-old. She uttered two words: "World class." It had been that, too.

From the first rally, you can generally tell how Robson will perform, how high her levels of confidence are and, on first sighting, there was a real eagerness about her which was highly encouraging. Taking on Miles Maclagan to coach her on a temporary basis during the grass court campaign had had a settling effect after the departure in May of Zeljko Krajan. The Croatian had been appointed to her team just before the 2012 US Open but departed after a few months with the rather blunt assessment that Robson's head was not in the sport as much as he felt it ought to be. They were hard words, he was not for retracting and Robson responded to them with an emboldened sense of desire.

Maclagan had already been seen to work hard to stiffen the left-hander's serve, which can be such a weapon. Against Kirilenko, she was especially effective with the slice out wide to the forehand which allowed her to spin the ball into the open court. But there were collywobbles, too.

Serving for the match at 5-4 in the second set, Robson had to stop the serve no fewer than five times because of a wonky ball toss. ("If you've seen me play before," she said, "that's nothing new,

It was a tougher day at the office for fellow Brits Tara Moore (top), who pushed Kaia Kanepi hard, and Heather Watson (bottom), who was ousted by the promising Madison Keys

unfortunately. It's something I'm working on.") She looked heavy-legged as she tried to will herself around the court and hit through her shots. And yet, she closed out the match almost despite herself. Given an easy mid-court ball on match point, she hit a looping, slightly mishit forehand that looked to be going wide. She paused and looked around the court waiting for the "out" call. It never came. She threw up her hands and shrugged, almost in disbelief.

"I thought I could win. I didn't expect to win," Robson said after her fourth victory against a top-10 player. "I thought if I go out there and play well and try to dominate from the start, keep the first-serve percentage high, I would give myself the best chance to win. That's what I was trying to focus on and that's what I managed to do."

There are very few players in the game whose ball-striking is as clean as the British teenager's. If she is in the right position, she more often than not plays the right shot. We have seen her go blow-for-blow with Grand Slam champions and leave them struggling to keep pace. A committed Robson is, potentially, a hugely successful Robson.

It was a shame for the locals that Heather Watson could not match Robson's form but, then again, she was up against it in the forbidding shape of the 18-year-old Madison Keys from the United States, a player of real promise. Watson did what she could on No.2 Court but Keys, with a serve

that will rip through the best defences in the years ahead, was simply stronger in every department and won 6-3, 7-5. Watson did well to have been competing at all so soon after her recovery from glandular fever, which can knock the stuffing out of the sturdiest souls.

Serena Williams did not mess around on her 2013 SW19 bow. She dismissed Mandy Minella of Luxembourg in the space of a not particularly strenuous lunch hour and insisted that she did not

feel invincible. In *The Times*, Giles Smith wrote: "Of course, this was Williams, meaning that, even during a routine overhauling, you still got the cloudy anger, the sense of an apocalyptic storm about to break, the dark moments of self-composure with her back to the court – not to mention the bringing of the thumb and forefinger of one hand to the temples in operatic despair, a gesture not often seen outside Pre-Raphaelite paintings. There is no greater player on the women's circuit, no better creator of drama and no one, surely, who you would rather be watching at any moment."

What made Novak Djokovic contented was his steady performance in the first round against Florian Mayer, the German whose style could make monkeys of a lot of folk. Mayer likes to take a big swing at the ball, to throw in a drop shot at unexpected moments and to bring out the dive every now and again. There were patches when he played very well indeed, but one of the differences between good players and great players is that great players play great tennis a lot longer and a lot more often.

(Above) *Despite being soundly beaten by Serena Williams, Mandy Minella of Luxembourg didn't stop smiling on Centre Court*

(Right) *James Blake began his 13th Wimbledon Championships with a first round win over Thiemo De Bakker*

Digital Wimbledon

Whether they are checking the scores around the courts, following live blogs or taking photos of their favourite players, the sight of people using mobile phones and tablets around the Grounds has become a familiar feature of the modern Wimbledon. And as the world continues to innovate at ever-more frightening speeds – with apps for everything from finding your car keys to what to put in your daily smoothie – sporting events, and Wimbledon in particular, have to keep step with those innovations to meet as many different audiences, in as many different ways, as possible.

In 2013 the first-ever official Wimbledon iPad app was launched, which aimed to present a unique view of The Championships for the digital user. Using aerial photography of the grounds as the navigation tool, and designed to replicate the beauty and tradition of Wimbledon in an iPad environment, the app featured 360 degree panoramic photography, videos and time-lapse cameras, as well as in-depth scoring and results information, photos, videos and more.

As well as iPhone and android apps, a mobile website, and of course the award-nominated *www.wimbledon.com*, Wimbledon 2013 had a prolific presence on social media, with tremendous growth on Facebook, Instagram, Google+, Twitter and YouTube, as well as two Chinese social media feeds. In total there were 19.6 million unique users of the various official Wimbledon digital platforms, 6.6 million Wimbledon-related tweets and 30 million Wimbledon-related interactions on Facebook.

Fans snatch pictures of Roger Federer on their mobile phones as the seven-time Wimbledon champion makes his way back from a practice session on one of the outside courts

WIMBLEDON IN NUMBERS

O Number of points lost by Serena Williams on serve in the first set of her 6-1, 6-3 win against Mandy Minella.

Thus, the No.1 seed dispatched Mayer 6-3, 7-5, 6-4 yet found his thoughts again drifting to his former coach Jelena Gencic, who had passed away during his recent campaign at the French Open. Djokovic was denied the victory he wanted at Roland Garros – in a spell-binding five-set defeat to Rafael Nadal – that would have acted as a tribute to his mentor. There were smiles and reminiscences on the day he took his initial step on another Grand Slam trail.

"She [Gencic] was a very special lady in my life," Djokovic said. "She was like my second mother, my mentor, somebody that has taught me a lot about sport, about life in general. I inherited that big passion and love towards tennis from her, because I didn't have anybody in my family who played it. Also at that time when I was growing up in Serbia, tennis was not really a popular sport. So she was the one that really has taught me a lot of nice things and gave me the right direction."

For every move in the right direction came news of one that would not be celebrated in the same fashion. With her 6-4, 6-2 defeat to Olga Puchkova of Russia, the Dutch girl Arantxa Rus lost her 17th consecutive match on tour, matching the losing run of American Sandy Collins in the mid-1980s. In the 13 defeats in 2013, Rus had won two sets. These things happen. We hope to see her back and flourishing again in 2014.

Novak Djokovic took his time to get going during his opening win

Sign of the times

The Aorangi practice courts at Wimbledon are very popular among spectators, not least because they give ardent fans the opportunity to ask for autographs from their favourite players. Novak Djokovic (*above*) is always in high demand, as are Rafael Nadal and Andy Murray (*above right*). Serena Williams (*below*) is a dedicated autograph-signer, and Laura Robson (*far right*) also always takes the time to scribble her name for tennis fans.

DAY THREE
WEDNESDAY 26 JUNE

There had been no warnings, no notice. The day dawned as most others, with a few clouds scudding and a touch of humidity in the air. The courts were uncovered, the stewards went about their business, the ball boys and girls folded the towels with the usual precision, the groundstaff busied themselves with mowing, tending and caring. The gardens looked lovely.

Sergiy Stakhovsky celebrates what he described as the greatest win of his career

Within an hour of the start of play, Andy Murray was preparing to venture out onto No.1 Court, and Jo-Wilfried Tsonga would be on in a minute against Ernests Gulbis, a match where sparks were expected fly. Maria Sharapova was set to play Michelle Larcher De Brito, and then it would be time to go and watch Mr Federer, the defending champion, do his thing. Normal service on Centre Court. Or so we thought.

By the time it had all ended for the day, with the net posts taken down and the towels back in the laundry, we had endured some tales of the completely unexpected, and of a defending champion who had bitten the grass in a most extraordinary way. It was the day when we were reintroduced to the magic art of serve-and-volley tennis by the 27-year-old son of an oncologist from Ukraine.

Sergiy Stakhovsky has gained notoriety as something of a barrack-room lawyer for the underprivileged of the tennis world. As a member of the ATP Player Council, he was one of the first to applaud the decisions of the Grand Slam tournaments to increase their prize money allocations for those departing the majors in the early rounds." I would like to give a big HUG to @Wimbledon board.. exciting news..thank you very much gentlemen !!" he tweeted when the All England Club announced its prize money increases earlier this year. What better way of stating the case that players outside the top 100 are worthy of their place at the top earnings table than to defeat the golden arm.

By 8.15pm Stakhovsky had brought Federer's record run of 36 consecutive Grand Slam quarter-finals to a decisive end – and this after he had lost the first set on a tie-break. But an hour and a half later he was storming his way through the fourth, still charging to the net on gangly, coltish legs that seemed never to tire. At the end he fell on his back on the grass, a final collapse to end the day as Centre Court rose to applaud not just one of the great shocks, but a brilliant, and brilliantly unexpected, performance. "You follow the 24-hour rule and you don't panic," Federer said. "These things happen. I still have plans to come back here for many years to come."

Afterwards Stakhovsky could scarcely stop himself beaming, and with good reason. "Beating Roger on this court, where he is a legend, is a special place in my career," he said. "When you come here Roger Federer is on the cover of the Wimbledon book. You're playing the guy and you're playing the legend which is following him, who won it seven times. You're playing two of them. When you're beating one you still have the other who is pressing you. You keep thinking, 'Am I really beating him?'"

It had all started so well for the Swiss, who emerged to the usual champion's reception, not just applause and cheers, but swoons as a familiar old fuzzy-ball genius ambled out in his tailored tunic to face a player who had never before beaten a top-10 opponent. "Even though he had dominated Wimbledon recently doing so at times in long trousers and a blazer, I never felt confident when I saw that jacket," wrote Simon Barnes in *The Times*.

The underrated Stakhovsky was a fidgety, beanpole of a figure with a distinctive freedom to his shot-making. What made one really wonder if he could win this was his insatiable desire to attack. He also mixed lobs and drives and volleys, and if there were some signs of creakiness in Federer's game, even as he edged towards a first-set tie-break which he would take with an ace that oozed authority, it did not seem as if the Ukrainian would fold.

(Left) *Dignified in defeat, Roger Federer insisted that he hopes to return to The Championships for many years to come*

The flying Ukrainian

It was a performance of brilliance from Sergiy Stakhovsky to upset Roger Federer on Centre Court, the Ukrainian's flamboyant style bringing back memories of the golden age of serve-and-volley, risky business in today's era of big-hitting baseline battles.

At times in the opening two sets, perhaps, there was even a sense of a champion expecting rather too stately a ride in front of his home-from-home crowd, only to be surprised by an energetic and aggressive opponent who refused to wilt. Serving with great accuracy, Stakhovsky took the second set to another tie-break, raising his levels just as Federer seemed to waver, and closed out the set 7-5.

Still the expected surge failed to materialise. At 1-1 and 5-5 Stakhovsky continued to produce precise serve-and volley tennis, his stamina unfailing, his touch secure. Federer saved the first of two break points with an ace but could not save the second, and Stakhovsky had his first break of serve in the 26th game. Two minutes later he had the third set and was punching the air, eyes wide, starting to glimpse the outline of a defining high point in his 10-year career. The end came in a rush. The Ukrainian reached double match point; Federer saved the first, he missed a backhand on the second.

Maybe it was simple magic. "We're staying in the house of a lovely family and they have four kids," Stakhovsky told the BBC. "The night before I played Roger, they left a pot of chocolate spread in front of the door to our room with a sticker on it saying 'magic recipe for Sergiy'. I had a little bit of it in the morning so the kids were happy, and it worked. That's why I said it was magic and now I'm taking it every day because they believe in it."

Upsets are certainly not unusual in Grand Slam tennis, the thrill of competing on the biggest of stages often tending to bring out the best in the game's underdogs. But Federer was not the only superstar to exit The Championships on the tournament's third day. One of not quite the same magnitude, but a shock nonetheless, was the loss of Sharapova to Larcher De Brito, 6-3, 6-4 on No.2 Court. Sharapova seemed unnerved, admittedly, after taking a tumble in the early stages of the match. But that alone did not account for De Brito's drive and determination as the young Portuguese failed to give up the advantage.

Michelle Larcher De Brito held nothing back in her defeat of Maria Sharapova

While Caroline Wozniacki was ousted 6-2, 6-2 by Petra Cetkovska, the Czech qualifier who seized the day just as De Brito had done, pre-existing injuries did some damage to the draw too. The news came through that Victoria Azarenka could not compete in her second round match, and neither

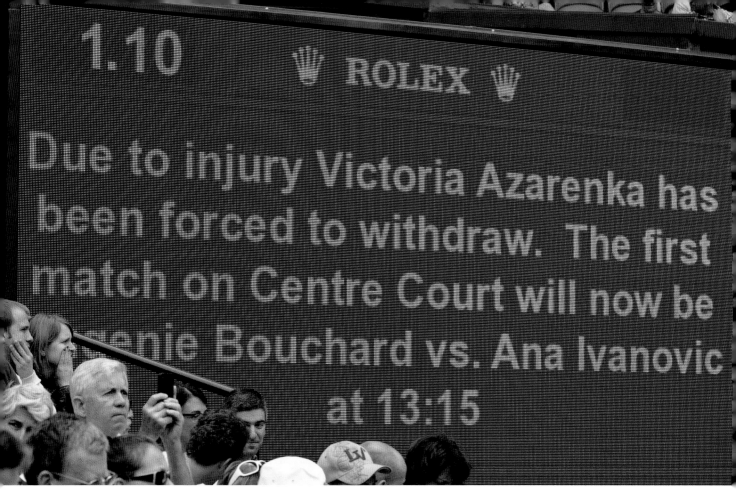

1.10 ♔ ROLEX ♔

Due to injury Victoria Azarenka has been forced to withdraw. The first match on Centre Court will now be Eugenie Bouchard vs. Ana Ivanovic at 13:15

Victoria Azarenka, Julien Benneteau **(left)**, Caroline Wozniacki **(below left)** and Jo-Wilfried Tsonga **(below)** departed The Championships far earlier than they had expected as injuries got the better of them

could Steve Darcis, Rafael Nadal's nemesis. Tsonga was down 2-1 in the fourth set to Gulbis and was forced to pull out, citing a knee problem that had prevented him from practising flat out for the previous three days; Marin Cilic, the Croatian who had reached the final of the Aegon Championships, could not make the court to face Kenny De Schepper of France; John Isner injured himself in the second game of his match against Adrian Mannarino

Dustin Brown produced a flamboyant performance to take out former champion Lleyton Hewitt in entertaining fashion

when his knee locked during a service motion ("like I have done 20 million times before with no problems"). Radek Stepanek retired in the second set against Jerzy Janowicz, and Yaroslava Shvedova of Kazakhstan – who had won a golden set at The Championships 2012 –hurt her knee and handed a walkover to Petra Kvitova, the 2011 champion.

Of course, with the loss of Federer and Nadal from his half, the pressure was turned up a notch on Murray, but the manner in which he swatted aside Lu Yen-Hsun on No.1 Court added to the sense that all was rather well. The British No.1's 6-3, 6-3, 7-5 victory was convincing against a player who had a strange habit of exhaling loudly before he played a shot. He was to be left gasping for breath.

The truth about the grass

'**Wacky Wednesday**', 'Weird Wednesday', 'What-on-earth-happened-on-Wednesday' – the first Wednesday of Wimbledon 2013 was an unusual one. "The court preparation has been to exactly the same meticulous standard as in previous years and it is well known that grass surfaces tend to be more lush at the start of an event," said Chief Executive Richard Lewis in a statement, as the world's press questioned the reasons for the large number of withdrawals. "The factual evidence, which is independently checked, is that the courts are almost identical to last year, as dry and firm as they should be, and we expect them to continue to play to their usual high quality."

Head groundsman Neil Stubley confirmed he and his team had made no changes to their methods. "You normally find that the first day or so of the grass court season, the grass is a little bit slippery purely because the leaf is still quite young and it has a little bit of moisture in it," he explained.

As several players maintained that the events of the day had nothing to do with the condition of the grass courts, what it proved instead is how important it will be for there to be an extra week's gap between the French Open and Wimbledon when The Championships are moved back a week from 2015. The three weeks will not only give players the time to recover from lingering injuries sustained during the grind of the clay court season, but will also afford them a greater opportunity to compete on grass in the run-up to Wimbledon.

Head groundsman Neil Stubley (*above*) explained that there had been no changes in the preparation of the grass courts at Wimbledon, they were made ready in the usual meticulous fashion

DAY FOUR
THURSDAY 27 JUNE

Taking St Mary's Walk back into the Club on the first Thursday of The Championships, you expected to meet Roger Federer or Rafael Nadal or Maria Sharapova or Victoria Azarenka or Jo-Wilfried Tsonga coming in the other direction, bidding you a hearty 'good day'. Instead, it all seemed a little empty, unless of course you delighted in royalty, in which case HRH The Duchess of Cornwall was in the house, chatting animatedly with the armed forces and a platoon of players lined up to greet her. The French seemed especially tickled that Richard Gasquet was in the welcoming line, and were stacked on the stairs with their cameras to capture the moment.

A sense of 'pinch me I'm dreaming' still pervaded the premises because some pretty nifty champions had bade their farewells. It was one of those days when you took a deep breath, looked a little more intently at the draw sheet and began to work out with more certainty (though not too much given the excesses of the first three days) who might end up playing whom as the tournament plot thickened.

In the bottom half of the ladies' draw, for instance, any one of a Puig, Birnerova, Stephens, Cetkovska, Bartoli, Giorgi, Knapp, Larcher De Brito, Kvitova, Makarova, Suarez Navarro, Bouchard, Dolonc, Flipkens, Cornet or Pennetta would make it to the final. History — and bucket-loads of it — awaited one of these ladies.

Those who had previously indulged in the slaughter of the less-than-innocents tried to get their heads around their achievements ("I didn't face a break point in my first 11 service games against Roger Federer on Centre Court at Wimbledon, wow," Sergiy Stakhovsky said) and prepare for what they knew would be an assignment with a far greater degree of difficulty the following day.

HRH The Duchess of Cornwall met, among others, Virginia Wade, John McEnroe and Tim Henman before taking her seat on Centre Court

"It is all a bit strange that so many top players lost," Novak Djokovic, a survivor thus far, said. "The lower-ranked players have an extra motivation, they have nothing to lose on the big stage and I needed to be extra careful. With the roof closed, it's a bit slower than I expected and I took some time to adjust. My game is there. I need to capitalise a little better on my opportunities."

This was Djokovic in the aftermath of a 7-6(2), 6-3, 6-1 success over Bobby Reynolds, the qualifier from the United States who wanted to relish his first and, quite possibly, only appearance on the grandest stage of them all, and fought for all his worth. Reynolds came into the match not exactly a lamb to the slaughter but, ranked 156 places behind Djokovic and with little prospect of narrowing the gap, the 30-year-old looked happy enough to be sharing the same stage as his illustrious opponent.

He hung in there, though. He saved two break points in the fifth game, but had few clues himself as to how to put pressure on Djokovic. It was not until the 10th game that the man from Cape Cod held to love – no mean feat against the best returner in the men's game. Still, he took him to a tie-break, and there Djokovic went up a level, clinching it with his sixth ace, always a definitive statement, a full point of intent.

And there were more. Djokovic was looking frighteningly strong in the shot, moving freely, and had that relaxed air about him which makes opponents left in the draw wonder just what he has still to offer. Plenty. There might have been none of the net-charging heroics of the Stakhovsky-Federer thriller on the same court the night before, but there was chilling power and precision – the Serb's trademarks.

His serve did not click so ominously in the second set but he did what he had to, and started pulling away. But the American was going nowhere. This was his moment in the sun – or megawatt lighting. He had to save three break points to hold serve at the start of the second as the pressure mounted and the match took on the air of a sparring session.

Bernard Tomic was the last man standing for Australia (Lleyton Hewitt had gone down to Dustin Brown, the dreadlocked Jamaican-turned-German amid the Wednesday frolics) and is a very decent grass court player in his own right, a quarter-finalist in 2011.

Australia has the richest of traditions on the grass. You inevitably bump into greats like Neale Fraser, John Newcombe and Tony Roche in the thoroughfares of the All England Club and Rod Laver was in the Royal Box at times – legendary figures one and all. As acts to follow, they take some beating and Tomic is very different – a sturdy, angular, 6ft 5ins lad who plays the game in a manner unlike most people, all caresses and clever angles, spins and the ability to manoeuvre the ball to difficult places for opponents with adroit disguise.

Top seed Novak Djokovic was comprehensive and assured in his defeat of Bobby Reynolds in the second round

While Bobby Reynolds (*above*) was the last American man standing in the second round, Madison Keys (*right*) and Sloane Stephens (*above right*) are just two members of an abundant group of US talent in the women's game

State of the Union

While America's women are flourishing, with up-and-comers Sloane Stephens, Jamie Hampton and Madison Keys all ranked inside the WTA's top 50 alongside the Williams sisters at the time of The Championships 2013, it was not a tournament to remember for American men. The early exits of Sam Querrey, John Isner and Ryan Harrison, and Mardy Fish's absence, meant that, once James Blake had departed, Bobby Reynolds was the last man standing. His loss to Novak Djokovic in the second round resulted in there being no American man in the third round for the first time since 1912.

His father and coach John had been banned from the Grounds after an altercation with Thomas Drouet, a former hitting partner from France, in Madrid in the spring; so Tomic was having to deal with those circumstances as well as trying to move through the field. Against the veteran American James Blake, who had lost in the first round for the past four years so was making progress of a kind, Tomic had to be skilful – Court 18 was packed to the rafters and there was enough brilliance on show for Tomic to merit thoroughly his 6-3, 6-4, 7-5 victory.

He did still, though, resemble something of a little boy lost. "My dad's still here. As soon as I get back to the house, he tells me what I've done, what I need to do. He's still helped me a lot. He's my dad. He's still my coach. If I can pick up any advice from him, it's huge, because he knows my game the best. I think that's why I'm doing well, because I am listening to my dad a little more the past few weeks."

WIMBLEDON IN NUMBERS

41

Grand Slam singles appearances played by James Blake. His 41st major came to an end at the hands of Bernard Tomic.

Bernard Tomic, a former Wimbledon quarter-finalist, reacts joyfully to his win over James Blake on Court 18

Caroline Garcia of France did her best to ruffle Serena Williams but with little success

As for missing fathers, there was no sign of Richard Williams around the Grounds in 2013, which did seem very strange. Often we would stop to talk – usually about how lovely the flower arrangements were – but Serena without her father, or mother for that matter, at a major championship felt a little peculiar. There was nothing wrong with her tennis, it seemed, although a 6-3, 6-2 victory over Caroline Garcia of France was very much closer than the scoreline would indicate.

Garcia had once been selected by no less an authority on women's tennis than Andy Murray for future greatness and you could see why – a 19-year-old with a terrific serve, a swipey flat forehand kill shot that reminded, a touch, of Steffi Graf. "She's incredibly promising, she does everything well," Serena said of her opponent. What of Williams – was she a better player now, or 10 years ago? "I wouldn't have wanted to play me at 21 or 31," she replied. Enough said.

There was a rare occurrence indeed when Michael Llodra, the Frenchman known for his personality traits, withdrew from his singles match against Andreas Seppi of Italy having lost the first set but returned later that day to play doubles with his partner Nicolas Mahut, only for their opponents, the Czechs Jan Hajek and Jaroslav Levinsky, to stop play in the first set with Levinsky hurt. Llodra has a track record of pulling out during singles matches, having previously done it on 31 occasions. By comparison, Federer has never done so.

The pride of Japan, Kei Nishikori, gave travelling fans plenty to cheer about with a straightforward win over Leonardo Mayer

Date with history

There are tennis players, and then there's Kimiko Date-Krumm. The extraordinary 42-year-old became the oldest woman to advance to the third round of Wimbledon in the Open era with her 6-4, 7-5 victory over Romania's Alexandra Cadantu on Day Four.

"I'm very happy. And especially I love Wimbledon. I have many good memories here. I have good results here," the popular Japanese player said. "So very special for me. So I'm very happy to be in the third round, even though I'm 42. I think it is amazing. So I cannot believe it. But this year I skipped the clay court season. I didn't play. I tried to focus on the grass."

Having last reached the third round at SW19 at the more usual age of 25, the 1996 Wimbledon semi-finalist rallied away in her inimitable style to set up a meeting with defending champion Serena Williams. In fact, it was after Wimbledon in 1996 that Date-Krumm took time off the tour to do 'normal things' such as get married, but ever since her return she has been a fearsome proposition. "When I came back I was enjoying it very much, even if I was losing. I have a lot of passion. I like a challenge," she said. And the secret behind her success? Regular cups of Chinese tea.

DAY FIVE
FRIDAY 28 JUNE

N

ot in the Open era of tennis had the top 10 in both the ladies' and men's singles fared as badly as they had in the first five days of these Championships. Only half of the best of the best were still competitive; the rest were hanging their heads.

Grigor Dimitrov found himself on the back foot during his loss to Grega Zemlja

"The newspapers are there in the locker room and, with some of the headlines and stuff, it is not that helpful," Andy Murray said. At least Murray had reached the sanctuary of the first weekend with his dignity intact, a 6-2, 6-4, 7-5 victory over Tommy Robredo of Spain completed under the Centre Court roof that was finally and firmly closed after the rain that had disrupted play in mid-afternoon.

There had been some pretty rum goings-on in the morning, one that was dark of hue and damp in nature. The draw was a bit behind because the men's second round had not been completed and third round matches were slated. One of those halted on Thursday in a tricky spot involved Grigor Dimitrov, the rising star from Bulgaria who had defeated Novak Djokovic on clay in Madrid in May provoking a firestorm of interest, and the rustic-looking Slovenian, Grega Zemlja. Dimitrov had to resume 9-8 down in the fifth having already saved a couple of match points. This was a situation that would have considerable bearing on the Bulgarian's character.

Maria Sharapova was on No.3 Court to support her boyfriend Dimitrov – the sunglasses didn't fool anyone. She had had an unhappy experience a couple of days earlier of conditions such as these and how they gave rise to tension and mistrust. Dimitrov immediately found himself 0-30 down but recovered to 30-30 before a nasty slip put him on his backside and offered Zemlja a third match point. The Bulgarian walked to his chair and sat down, muttering about the conditions which left the umpire, Ali Nili, to clamber down and test the court with the tried and trusted method of a swipe of the back of his hand. With the players refusing to budge from their chairs, the crowd was informed that play would not restart until the drizzle, as thin as it was, had stopped. Ten minutes passed until it was decided they could begin warming up again and, after three minutes of such to and fro, there was enough adrenalin in Bulgarian veins for Dimitrov to save the match point as Zemlja netted his forehand return.

A fourth match point came and went and then a fifth as Dimitrov held his nerve, and eventually his serve. And when he forced a break point in the next game, indications were that he would go on to victory. But Zemlja, a doughty foe, resisted with a giant first serve and, after holding, moved ahead 30-0 on the Bulgarian's serve. Dimitrov showed good resolve to recover to 30-30 but missed a backhand to donate Zemlja a sixth match point. This time, the Slovenian got his return into play and, in what would prove the defining rally, there were net-cords from both before Zemlja ripped a brilliant forehand pass to secure a third round berth. Dimitrov was rightly crushed. Sharapova looked forlorn.

As for Robredo, Simon Briggs in the *Daily Telegraph* described his experience of playing Murray as "like running into a 6ft 3ins threshing machine". At the end of the match, Simon Barnes in *The Times* declared boldly: "Andy Murray is going to win this tournament. On all three of his [playing] days, Murray played tennis and mostly looked like a champion. Not a potential champion, but a player with the swagger, the touch and the assurance of the man in charge. The real point is that Murray has never looked better in this tournament and he looked pretty good last year when he was the runner-up."

Maria Sharapova (top) was on No.3 Court to lend her support to boyfriend Dimitrov, but he could not prevent Zemlja (bottom) celebrating victory

Robredo may have brought a rugged resourcefulness to his tennis, but he simply did not have the ammunition to overpower Murray in a slugging contest. And that, it appeared, would have been the only realistic way to win. The first few points set the tone, producing lengthy rallies in which Murray seemed to be working at around three-quarter intensity, not quite certain where he should jab or unleash. Yet the ball was fizzing off his racket so venomously that Robredo had to sprint and hustle just to stay in the point. Above all, Murray's signature stroke – the two-fisted backhand down the line – was in the sweetest groove imaginable. And this was good to see for it had been a little hit and miss in previous engagements.

When asked, after his victory was completed, whether he had felt less pressure as a result of being a Grand Slam winner, he replied: "From what I've heard, people are putting even more pressure on me because of the nature of the draw. It would be easier if we just take one match at a time. There are a lot of tough players left, and some young guys trying to make a name for themselves."

Andy Murray
covered the court
with deftness
during his three-set
win over Spain's
Tommy Robredo

WIMBLEDON IN NUMBERS

1999
The last time two British players won singles matches on Centre Court on the same day, when Tim Henman and Greg Rusedski did so

Lendl, attempting to sum up the position and not hoist more on his protégé, said about the events of the first week: "It happens all the time. In Paris, the two guys in the semis [Djokovic and Rafael Nadal] and everyone thinks it's the finals – sometimes your draw opens up, seeds lose. I would not call Andy's draw by any means open. Both Rafa and Roger lost but they didn't lose because the other guys can't play; they lost because the other guys played very well and you can see how closely they are tagged in the next round. It's like in golf, someone shoots a 62 and they don't often follow it with a 64.

"The guys who beat the top guys, there's more requirements on them and attention they are not used to and a lot of times they don't make it through the next match. It has happened and those players are good players. You definitely cannot relax, it has happened, it will happen somewhere again when seeds lose and, though in some people's eyes it is open, in my mind it is not open, it is still very difficult."

Lendl's viewpoint was endorsed when Sergiy Stakhovsky (conqueror of Roger Federer) and Dustin Brown (conqueror of Lleyton Hewitt) discovered that there was no second bolt of lightning. Stakhovsky lost to Jurgen Melzer, the Austrian who was simply too effective on the return of serve, and Brown lost all of his fizz when he faced the French left-hander Adrian Mannarino. Was it coincidence that, whereas they had profited against right-handers, coming up against a lefty presented an entirely unfathomable test?

(Above) American Alison Riske continued to lead a charmed life on grass, defeating Urszula Radwanska in three sets

(Below) Jurgen Melzer (left) took four sets to end Sergiy Stakhovsky's run at SW19, while Alexandr Dolgopolov (right) had a much more straightforward win

One of those apparently unaffected by all the mayhem was David Ferrer, he of the tireless tenacity. The Spaniard, a Grand Slam finalist for the first time in Paris a month before, defeated his compatriot Roberto Bautista Agut 6-3, 3-6, 7-6(4), 7-5. Ferrer's instincts frequently seemed defensive – in the prevailing conditions it was no surprise – and there were large portions of the match where, had you thrown a towel over the scoreboard, you would have said he was being played off the court. Does Ferrer have a volley? There was previous little evidence that he knew the shot was still legal.

He won, though, as did Jerzy Janowicz of Poland on his debut on Centre Court in a 7-6(6), 6-3, 6-4

Mariana Duque-Marino **(above)** *was overpowered by Laura Robson on Centre Court; David Ferrer* **(below)** *was not hampered by a rain delay*

victory over Spaniard Nicolas Almagro, the 15th seed.

There was a convincing victory in the ladies' event for Laura Robson, 6-4, 6-1 over Mariana Duque-Marino, the world No.117, but just the kind of 'who is she?' opponent that has tended to act as a banana skin to the British player's ambitions in events past. "A country desperate for contenders to get behind at its home Grand Slam fervently wants Robson to succeed, with the assembly getting right behind her when awkward passages presented themselves, cheering the winners and gasping in horror at the mistakes," wrote Mike Dickson in the *Daily Mail*. As Robson herself reflected, "We're living it together."

The court covers, complete with logo, were well-used on Day Five at The Championships as the rain came down at intermittent intervals, forcing spectators to arm themselves with umbrellas

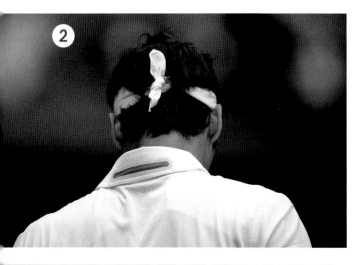

Getting ahead

Ask any tennis player and they will tell you that keeping their hair out of their eyes is one of the most important things you can do. So it's no surprise that the game's stars go in for all sorts of headgear. There is the humble bandana, as favoured by Roger Federer ❷ and David Ferrer ❸, or a simpler version, as sported by Serena Williams ❶. Britain's Elena Baltacha ❺ tends to use a visor, while the flamboyant Bethanie Mattek-Sands ❻ kept her colourful locks contained in a regulation baseball cap. But there are those seemingly unconcerned about keeping their hair in check. Dustin Brown ❹ prefers to let his dreads fly behind him, while Redfoo ❼, the popstar and boyfriend of Victoria Azarenka, accessorises with sunglasses instead.

DAY SIX
SATURDAY 29 JUNE

The entrance was timed to perfection. A montage of the successful British Olympians and Paralympians from London 2012 had been shown to the crowd on Centre Court. They had received and acknowledged the reception rightly afforded them. It was also Armed Forces Day and the noise grew ever more deafening as we rose to salute the soldiers, sailors and airmen and women in whom our pride was

unequivocal. We could tell by the meticulous and courteous manner with which they went about showing the patrons to their seats at Wimbledon how professional they were in a rather more alarming field of action.

Andy Murray (above) takes his seat among fellow Olympic and Paralympic medallists such as Sir Chris Hoy (right) on a surprise visit to the Royal Box

But wait. "Haven't we forgotten someone?" Sue Barker of the BBC asked. A nice little piece of pre-planned improvisation and here came Andy Murray, members' badge pinned to his right lapel, perfectly-knotted tie. He looked a little sheepish, because that is the way of the man, managed a discreet wave and shook hands with as many of those he could reach without leaning too far across the front row. Dignity and discretion in equal portion.

Murray was having a day off in playing terms but the crowd's response when he made his appearance was truly heart-warming. They were glad to see him more as a person than as a player, and this was defining indeed. "Normally when you go out there, you are walking onto the court, and you don't really get the chance to enjoy that so much," he said. "Going in as a spectator was a bit different. My job is to deal with everything that goes with playing at Wimbledon but I know the crowd is right there with me and that is a great boost." He would be back in his work clothes the following Monday.

A couple of floors down from where his old chum was receiving his acclaim, Jamie Baker had decided that his career as a professional player was over. He had not received a wild card in 2013, had not made it through Qualifying and felt that the time was right to bid farewell to the sport. I had first met him on a bus back from Flushing Meadows to Manhattan 10 years earlier. No one had done more to make more of themselves than Baker. And he faced up to the decision about leaving as solidly as he had everything else, be it triumph, trial or tribulation. "I have no doubt that the time is right for a new challenge and I am ready to test the phenomenal life skills that the tennis world has helped me to develop," he wrote. "Resilience, application, responsibility, independence, leadership, hard work. Values, characteristics and personality traits can be permanent and those are the areas I am ready to take into another walk of life."

Hopefully, those decisions are some way off for Murray and will not enter Laura Robson's mind for at least another decade. What a prosperous period that might be if she could sustain the form of the opening week in SW19. Well, make that the last two sets of her first week, for the opening few minutes of her match against Marina Erakovic of New Zealand on No.2 Court suggested that the party might be pooped in a particularly disappointing manner.

During the 22 minutes it took Erakovic to race into a one-set lead those who had brought Union flags to wave were surreptitiously hiding them under their seats. And the middle-aged man who had spent the previous match between Serbia's Viktor Troicki and Mikhail Youzhny of Russia with the British flag painted on his face appeared more than a trifle embarrassed.

Petra Kvitova, the 2011 champion, battled her way to victory over Ekaterina Makarova

When the turnaround came it was a joint effort born of Robson's tenacity and the goodwill pouring from the stands. As the match, almost imperceptibly, turned her way she began to use the crowd to her advantage. Not least in sealing a topsy-turvy second set from 3-5 down which turned in her favour not necessarily because of the pugnacity of her own strokes but due to Erakovic suddenly being consumed with nerves. Well, it is not every day you have the chance to become the first woman from New Zealand to reach the last 16 of The Championships. What had appeared to be a friendly racket in her right hand seemed in a trice to carry all the weight of an anvil.

Robson happily plotted her way through to the second week, winning 1-6, 7-5, 6-3 to bring an end to 15 years of waiting for a British representative to achieve that feat in the ladies' draw. The family was there in force, too, for though Kathy, Laura's mother, was away in Greece, her father Andrew was in the crowd and her brother Nick, working as part of the groundstaff during his holidays from Durham University, was given leave to down tools on Court 17 and join the throng on No.2 Court.

Well done Laura!

Laura Robson's three-set victory over Marina Erakovic – willed on by the passionate No.2 Court crowd which included her father and her brother who was working at Wimbledon as a member of the groundstaff – propelled her into the last 16 of the ladies' singles, the first British woman to reach that stage since Sam Smith in 1998.

WIMBLEDON IN NUMBERS

600

Career singles wins for Serena Williams as she defeated Kimiko Date-Krumm 6-2, 6-0 on Centre Court.

"They [the crowd] were so great towards the end of the second and the beginning of the third set. I didn't give them much to cheer before that. They were amazing and I thought they helped a lot," Robson said.

Even more encouragingly, Robson's increasing maturity and Grand Slam experience – this was her fifth appearance in the main Wimbledon draw at just 19 – boded well for future editions.

Back on Centre Court – from where Murray had departed without actually watching a ball being struck – Bernard Tomic solidly despatched the former semi-finalist Richard Gasquet of France in four taut sets, 7-6(7), 5-7, 7-5, 7-6(5). The next two followed in relatively swift order, with Sabine Lisicki of Germany responding to the loss of the opening set against Australia's Samantha Stosur by bombing through the remaining two and then Novak Djokovic dropping only seven games to Jeremy Chardy of France, a daunting performance in every respect. As such, at 8.30pm, with the roof drawn shut, Serena Williams was moved from her expected place on No.1 Court (where David Ferrer and Alexandr Dolgopolov were involved in a decidedly topsy-turvy affair before the Spaniard prevailed in five sets) to the main theatre.

Whether or not Serena was affronted at having to play on No.1 Court at all, her 6-2, 6-0 obliteration of Kimiko Date-Krumm was very business-like. A word or two should be reserved for the Japanese, though, for Date-Krumm was 42, had made her debut in the tournament in 1989, had played in the semi-finals against Steffi Graf 17 years earlier, hit every shot with a beaming smile on her face, and was an everlasting credit to the game. The next day at Aorangi Park, I saw her practise against her coach and another hitter, barely miss a ball and revel in every minute.

Serena, though, was not interested in assisting the tennis equivalent of Help the Aged. Though broken when she served for the opening set, the match was over before anyone had really had time to get into it. This was her 600th career win, a remarkable testament in itself. "That's awesome," she said. "I had absolutely no idea. That feels really good. On Centre Court – what better place to win 600 matches?"

"I'm finally starting to feel a little better. I had such a long clay court season and my first match I felt was a little awkward, so I'm getting there. I always like to peak towards the end. It's unbelievable playing here on Centre Court under the roof – I don't think it gets better for me than playing under a closed roof on grass."

There was American company for Serena in the shape of Sloane Stephens, the player who had defeated her in the quarter-finals of the Australian Open in January. Stephens, the No.17 seed, had not previously been beyond the third round at this tournament but a 7-6(3), 0-6, 6-4 victory over Petra Cetkovska of the Czech Republic was reward for a strong display. The result prevented the American from joining the casualty list that had inspired her to label the first week of The Championships "Wimblegeddon".

(Far left) Visitors to the Grounds have a break before being allowed to take their seats on court

The fairytale continued for 19-year-old Wimbledon debutante Monica Puig of Puerto Rico as she beat Eva Birnerova to reach the fourth round

The Wimbledon

Master Plan

In April 2013, the All England Club published the Wimbledon Master Plan, the Club's vision for the future development of the Grounds. AELTC Chairman Philip Brook outlines that vision.

What is the Wimbledon Master Plan trying to achieve?

"Firstly, to be true to our mission statement, and to maintain Wimbledon as the finest stage in world tennis. Secondly, to address the operational needs of the tournament both now and looking forward 10-15 years, and crucially the need to create more space. And thirdly, the original Long Term Plan talked about 'tennis in an English garden'. That is a theme we will embed in this plan also."

What are the cornerstones of the plan?

"Central to the thinking has been putting a new fixed and retractable roof on No.1 Court. It will allow 11,500 tennis fans to watch the action on No.1 Court irrespective of the weather and it will give our broadcasters a second court to televise at all times. The whole northern end of the Grounds will have a very different feel, it will be very green, with a new main entrance and a much more inviting sense of welcome. The Aorangi Pavilion will move underground, with potentially two new indoor courts and new Championships courts.

The southern end of the Grounds is very congested, so we propose to move Court 12 further south and space out the original two banks of four courts. We would like to create new areas for players to relax, significantly larger changing and rehabilitation facilities, and also a new indoor centre and clay court area across Somerset Road."

What are the next steps?

"We've created a vision. It will evolve and there is no set end date. But our expectation is that the new No.1 Court roof will be available for use for the 2019 Championships. It's very exciting."

(*Far left*) The Wimbledon Master Plan sets out a vision to maintain 'tennis in an English garden', with increased open space, improved access to courts, and new underground facilities

Central to the plan is the building of a new fixed and retractable roof on No.1 Court, aimed to be completed for The Championships 2019

DAY SEVEN

MONDAY 1 JULY

A new month had dawned but it seemed as if June – and its disorderly climax – did not want to loosen its grip. The second Monday of The Championships is the tennis equivalent of 'moving day' in golf's The Open Championship in that 16 people are removed from the draw and all those first-week dreams, replenished by a day of rest to think about them in the solitude of one's back garden or hotel suite, are dashed.

Sabine Lisicki celebrates the win of her life, out-hitting Serena Williams at her own game

It was rather appropriate then that the Royal Box would be filled with talk of hooks and shanks, niblicks and wedges, bunkers and out of bounds. A steady stream of golfers took their places: the great American Jack Nicklaus, the proud owner of three grass tennis courts in his back garden in North Palm Beach, Florida; Ernie Els, who would be defending his Open crown at Muirfield later that month; England's Ian Poulter; and Paul McGinley, the Irishman who holed a 10-footer in 2002 to secure a European victory in the Ryder Cup at The Belfry.

As far as we know, there is no photographic evidence of Serena Williams having swung a golf club but her talents with a racket are undeniable. In the fourth round, she met Sabine Lisicki of Germany, a player who has a passion for this surface every bit as profound as that of Boris Becker, her esteemed compatriot and three times the champion. Lisicki had told Barbara Rittner, the German Fed Cup captain, that she felt something good was going to happen to her on this day. She could not have known quite how good it would be. It would be front-page good.

There had not been one reputable judge of the game who had not picked Williams to win the ladies' singles; she had dominated the game in the past year – the odd stumble, true, but that was about it. 'Imperious' hardly did her justice. But in Lisicki, she faced someone who did not melt when the first serve came thudding down, who refused to countenance inferiority, who stood shoulder to shoulder and forehand to forehand. Lisicki gave as good as she got and that, as it turned out, was good enough for a splendid victory.

The score was 6-2, 1-6, 6-4 and if you wondered how it happened, these statistics might help: Lisicki lost only three fewer points than Williams, served more aces (10-7), won 14 of her 16 net approaches and hit 10 more winners (against only two more errors) than Serena. Repeat: Lisicki had 10 more winners (35-25) than her opponent, who is generally regarded as the most potent ball-striker in the history of the women's game. Also, consider this: three times before 2013, Lisicki had beaten the reigning French Open champion at Wimbledon – Svetlana Kuznetsova, Li Na and Maria Sharapova. The winner of the 2013 French Open? Serena Williams.

After dropping her first set of the tournament, Williams – as she so often does – seemed to toggle a switch. She began dialling in her serves and blasting away, punctuating her winners with violent cries of "Come on". They are enough to shake the most rigid of foundations. In barely the time it takes to polish off a plate of cucumber sandwiches, she won the second set and was up 3-0 in the third after a run of nine consecutive games.

Well, we thought, that was a good try from Sabine. See you next year. And then Williams missed a series of balls, including an overhead shank befitting a club player, and Lisicki stopped missing. At 4-4, Williams played a shaky service game, and the adventure seemed to drain from her. As the coaches say, she played not to lose. Lisicki took a deep breath, overcame a few nerves and served it out.

The idea that a British player might still be standing in both the men's and ladies' draw come fourth round day was invigorating – it had not happened since 1998, when Sam Smith and Tim Henman carried local fortunes. Robson faced Kaia Kanepi of Estonia, a player who had reached this stage of a Grand Slam four times before and had not been beaten. Indeed, she had been a quarter-finalist here (having qualified) in 2010 and had been as high as No.15 in the world a year later. She was trim and strong, looking better than she had for some time, and Robson knew she would be in a battle.

It proved to be one that was beyond her. Equally tall and forceful in her groundstrokes, Kanepi was simply more physically mature, more precise in her movements. There always seemed to be a greater function about her whereas Robson looked a little tetchy and her movement was not what it needed to be. Indeed it was a rather hushed No.1 Court at times, even as Robson appeared to be on her way to taking the first set at 5-4 with a break of serve.

Williams admitted afterwards that she had the win on her racket but didn't take it

Not this time, though, as the Robson forehand began to lose its range at exactly the wrong moment. Having broken Kanepi's serve to love, Robson was suddenly yelping in frustration as she sent another mistimed clump beyond the baseline, with her opponent moving her from side to side with decisive effect. "At one point in the first set she [Robson] made a lunging attempt to retrieve a wide forehand drive that saw her topple very slowly into the tramlines like a Grenadier Guard heroically fainting on parade," wrote Barney Ronay in *The Guardian*.

Robson's moment came and went at 5-2 up in the tie-break. Helped by one double fault that hit the grass on Robson's side of the net, Kanepi reeled her in with an angler's efficiency to

Jack's back!

Golfing legend Jack Nicklaus explains his love of tennis and his passion for Wimbledon.

How different is Wimbledon from other sporting tournaments you have played at and been to?

"I think Wimbledon is sort of the [US] Masters of tennis. The quality of tennis and the quality of the facilities is unmatched anywhere in the world."

What is the best match you have seen at Wimbledon?

"The match I watched last year between Roger Federer and Julien Benneteau was a pretty unusual match. Roger was down two-sets-to-love and came back to win under the Centre Court roof with a late finish – I enjoyed that match. But there are obviously so many other matches. Going back through the years I watched Stan Smith defeat Ilie

Nastase in five sets in the 1972 final – and that's a lot of years ago! I also watched John Newcombe win here at Wimbledon."

What makes watching tennis at Wimbledon unique?

"It's a total contrast to what we have in the United States. I think that's why I enjoy coming over here so much because it is a unique way of watching sport. There's an amazing atmosphere here."

Are there any other players who stand out for you from Wimbledon's illustrious history?

"I enjoyed the era in the 1970s and 1980s with the likes of Bjorn Borg, John McEnroe and Jimmy Connors. Then, of course, along came Pete Sampras and Andre Agassi. I like Pete and know him a little bit, but I've never met Andre."

take it 8-6, and the set in 49 minutes. There was a moan of frustration from Robson, who suggested afterwards that she tried at times to play the perfect shot, to unleash her forehand a little too spectacularly, when in fact staying in the point was the better option.

Simon Barnes in *The Times* said of Robson's defeat: "The thing about teenagers is that they have lived for fewer than 20 years. It's important to bear that in mind when making judgements about them. Being a teenager is a bit like this summer: glorious but horribly brief periods of inspissated gloom and long stretches that can't make up their mind."

The men's event continued similarly to promote order and disorder in equal measure. There were no seismic shocks on what is known as Manic Monday, although a couple of names to reach the quarter-finals would take some becoming accustomed to. Lukasz Kubot, who

Tommy Haas could not disrupt Novak Djokovic's stride towards the last eight

defeated the French left-hander Adrian Mannarino, did not even have his own page in the ATP World Tour's media guide, so unknown was he, and suddenly we would have two Polish players in the quarter-finals with the assurance, given that they were to face each other, of one in the semi-finals. "It is magical," said Jerzy Janowicz, the second Polish victor on the men's side of the competition. Janowicz defeated Jurgen Melzer of Austria having lost the first set on Court 12, complaining that the conditions underfoot were a touch hazardous. "I slipped four times and that doesn't happen to me too often. These were bad conditions today, so many bad bounces," he said. To which the response should have been: "Welcome to grass, Jerzy."

Opposing Novak Djokovic was Tommy Haas, the standard-bearer for the mid-thirties male, with the peaked cap turned back to front in keeping with his youthful attitude to life. Haas had won more than 100 matches in Grand Slam tournaments, had been a Wimbledon semi-finalist four years ago and has a game which is so easy on the eye that it is not difficult to be lulled in by it. Djokovic won the first set commandingly but relaxed — mentally more than anything — to find himself a break down in the second.

At that change of ends, he yanked his shirt up over his head, so much so that it came apart in his hands (this man really does have superhuman strength). He sat there, contemplating his relatively naked position and determined that that was the end of that little bit of German fun.

WIMBLEDON IN NUMBERS

4 Reigning Roland Garros champions who have lost to Sabine Lisicki at Wimbledon. The German beat Svetlana Kuznetsova in 2009, Li Na in 2011, Maria Sharapova in 2012 and Serena Williams in 2013.

Some of Djokovic's retrieving from then on defied the expected laws of the grass court game — the wider he was drawn to the outer, greener reaches of the court, the more remarkable became his defensive capacities, so that he secured a 6-1, 6-4, 7-6(4) victory in a tie-break of breathtaking dimensions.

Andy Murray, meanwhile, defeated Mikhail Youzhny of Russia in three sets, 6-4, 7-6(5), 6-1. I bumped into Ivan Lendl a few minutes after the last shot was played. He said he hoped that was Murray's bad match out of the way.

Murray moves on

Andy Murray's three-set win over Mikhail Youzhny might not have been his greatest Centre Court performance – that was still to come – but it still left his Russian opponent on the floor.

A day in the life

From dawn to dusk, Wimbledon never sleeps. These photos show a day in the life of the southern courts and the view towards Centre Court, from midnight. The courts are covered until 7am, then cut, mowed and dressed for play at 11.30am. At 9.30pm they are re-covered and put to bed by the time darkness falls at 10pm.

DAY EIGHT
TUESDAY 2 JULY

Now there were eight protagonists remaining in the Ladies' Singles Championship, of whom two, Petra Kvitova and Li Na, had won a Grand Slam title, and a further two, Marion Bartoli and Agnieszka Radwanska, had played in a Wimbledon final – in 2007 in the case of the former, and in 2012 for the latter.

The departures of Victoria Azarenka and Maria Sharapova almost before the event had come off the blocks, and of Serena Williams in the 'where to turn?' cacophony of the second Monday, had left the tournament as wide open as it had been in years. Of those still participating, perhaps the arrival of Kirsten Flipkens of Belgium in the quarter-finals was the most appealing story of all.

Petra Kvitova rued many missed opportunities during her shock defeat to Belgian Kirsten Flipkens

In mid-2012, two days before she was due to have flown to Japan for a Fed Cup tie, she was discovered to have blood clots in her calf, four in total, and was told that had she stepped onto that plane it was not known what her condition would have been by the time the journey was over. It was, Flipkens discovered, a genetic condition, and she required blood thinners if she flew longer than three hours and had to wear compression socks. She said it was hard to deal with "but at least mentally I now know I'm safe".

At that stage, she said she had lost the financial support of the Belgian Federation and her ranking had dropped to No.262 – poor enough to miss out on the Qualifying Competition for The Championships 2012. Although she was on her own, she never lost faith or confidence. "My highest ranking had been 59 and I was 100 per cent certain I'd be in the top 50, which was the main thing that kept me going. I travelled on my own during last summer with no coach but my main sponsor was there and Kim Clijsters [former Grand Slam champion and world No.1] put herself out there and supported me.

"I had to go to tournaments myself. I did everything by myself, even if I was at home I was calling to some guys if they were able to play with me that day to practise. I had a rough year, the last half year was really tough. But I played great. Even in Quebec, when I won my first WTA title, I was there alone, and that gives you a lot of support mentally and physically."

Thus, Flipkens was one of the feel-good stories of The Championships, and how well she battled against Kvitova. The Belgian had glided almost invisibly through the draw but had reached this stage without dropping a set. That record disappeared rather swiftly against Kvitova, and the 23-year-old from the Czech Republic looked as if she might have a straightforward afternoon. But that's not really her style. If you think it's emotionally draining to be a British tennis fan, spare a thought for followers of Kvitova.

Flipkens had battled back from the discovery of life-threatening blood clots in mid-2012

Rolling back the years

John McEnroe
(*above*) and
Mansour Bahrami
(*below*) were
among the
famous faces
competing in
the Invitation
Doubles events

One of the thrills of attending The Championships is glimpsing top players from previous decades milling around the Grounds as they go about their work as TV commentators or full-time coaches. But there's even more excitement on the second Tuesday of the tournament when some of those former stars don their whites and step back on court to compete in the Ladies' and Gentlemen's Invitation Doubles and the Gentlemen's Senior Invitation Doubles.

Sixteen players compete in each of the three events, drawn into two round robin groups, with all participants selected at the Club's invitation.

Mansour Bahrami, of course, has turned his 'retirement' into an art form as the archetypal court jester, with the full range of humorous shots and cheeky skills, but the big attraction of 2013 was the return of John McEnroe, not with his old doubles partner, Peter Fleming, but with his younger brother Patrick. The McEnroes were in the fiercely contested Senior Invitation Doubles, which also featured Pat Cash, Fleming, Guy Forget, and Mark Woodforde to name but a few.

In the younger Invitation Doubles, the likes of Richard Krajicek, Greg Rusedski and Mark Philippoussis were in fine fettle, while the Ladies' Invitation Doubles featured Tracy Austin, Lindsay Davenport, Martina Hingis and Martina Navratilova among the 16 competitors.

No one on the women's tour has played more three-set matches than she has. She tends to win a lot of them but the statistics also tell you that she is deeply mercurial, often prone to lapses in concentration. As the match progressed, Kvitova became more reckless and attempted to shorten the points with explosive winners. Her plan did not work well because Flipkens was a wall, returning Kvitova's pummelling groundstrokes with a sapping backhand slice. Kvitova's legs began to look heavy and, at 4-4 in the final set, she crumpled. Flipkens won 4-6, 6-3, 6-4.

Agnieszka Radwanska (above) charges down a ball during her thrilling win over Li Na (below)

A heavily pregnant Clijsters was watching the match from her home in the United States. "Still drying my eyes :-))" she wrote on Twitter. "So proud of how [Flipkens] handled the big occasion for the first time!" She was not alone in that. The Belgians were as gobsmacked as they had been on the first day by the heroics of Steve Darcis.

And then there was a blissful match on Centre Court between Radwanska and Li Na, one that touched everyone who witnessed some, or all, of it. One of those fortunate to see each ball, Simon Barnes, reflected in *The Times* on a "feast of WWT (wonderful, wonderful tennis), of two talented and immensely smart competitors hitting with bewildering accuracy and playing points that you wished would go on forever — quite a lot of

WIMBLEDON IN NUMBERS

262

The ranking of Kirsten Flipkens 15 months ago, meaning she was ineligible for Wimbledon Qualifying.

them seemed to. Li saved six match points, five in the final game but reaching for victory was like reaching for the soap in the shower; forever slipping just out of reach. But Radwanska triumphed and is doing her bit to change the world with dramatic and startlingly confident tennis".

Li Na retained the ability to smile at everything, even after a 7-6(5), 4-6, 6-2 defeat. "It was pretty good really. At least better than the last two years. And also, you know, I prove another thing, prove so many things on the court. Yeah, like before I was never thinking I can come to the net as like today so many times. So at least now we have a job to do – me and Carlos [Rodriguez, her coach]. We know what we should do for next step. It's not bad, right? I mean, I come in I don't know how many times because today I didn't get any information." The moderator nudged a piece of paper in front of her and pointed to a line. "Oh, they say 71. Not bad. So I think maybe today I came to the net much more than my whole life."

Radwanska booked a semi-final spot against Sabine Lisicki who defeated Kaia Kanepi 6-3, 6-3, while the fourth semi-finalist was Bartoli, a 6-4, 7-5 victor against the last American, Sloane Stephens. With so many superior seeds already mown into the grass, there was an expectation that Stephens could add another one to their number. Yet it is on these occasions where, one assumes, a greater

Sabine Lisicki (below) became the first giant-killer to follow through on her upset, defeating Kaia Kanepi (below right) without difficulty

experience will be brought to bear, so while Bartoli hit deep and took away the angles, Stephens did not seem to have much of a theory in response. Serving at 4-5 in the first set, a slight drizzle began to fall and Bartoli – showing a little cunning – declined to play on at deuce. It may not have been in the true spirit of competition but the officials were seized and a two-hour interruption followed, enough time for Stephens to stew on her position.

"It would have been nice to finish that game. Coming back and serving at deuce, that's always going to be tough for anyone," Stephens reflected later. "Yeah, but you have just got to move on. I mean, things happen, like I said. You just keep working hard. You know, everyone gets their moment. You do what you have to do to win. And if that helps her, then she's got it down pat. Do what you have to do to win."

In the second set, Bartoli comforted herself like a 12-year veteran, going through her routines between points – quirky as they are – and betraying little emotion. Stephens looked the part of the 20-year-old learner-player, taking more risks than the situation demanded, approaching the net with small steps rather than entirely confident in her movement. After recovering from a 3-5 deficit which roused the crowd, Stephens had all kinds of opportunities to level the match. Instead, forehands sailed long, backhands curled wide, first serves hit the net. Bartoli won 6-4, 7-5. It was time for Stephens to return to her tennis education and next time, surely, she would be better prepared for any situation.

During the day, I had walked with Novak Djokovic through the tunnel that links Aorangi Park and the front entrance of the Club, by means of appraising his demeanour on the day before the men's quarter-final in which he would play Tomas Berdych. He had said he was a big nature lover and enjoyed spending time in Wimbledon's parks. "I am happy out there thinking my own thoughts," he said. "My game is very, very good right now."

Marion Bartoli (below left) was as focused as she has ever been during her straight-sets win over American Sloane Stephens (below)

DAY NINE
WEDNESDAY 3 JULY

S ir Alex Ferguson and I have had our moments. In 1993, during my spell as football correspondent of the *Daily Mail*, he threatened to leave me behind at Istanbul airport after a particularly tempestuous European Cup match (I was the straggler who did not hear the last call for the flight home to Manchester), and when I dashed breathlessly onto the plane, after a right telling-off from the manager in front of the entire squad, you could have heard a pin drop.

Andy Murray showed great strength to come back from two sets to love down to beat Fernando Verdasco

The same was the case on Centre Court as Andy Murray, watched from the Royal Box by Sir Alex, served out to love for a place in the Wimbledon semi-finals for the fifth year in succession. There was a momentary pin-dropping pause and then the old place blew its lid. Murray had defeated Fernando Verdasco of Spain 4-6, 3-6, 6-1, 6-4, 7-5, a match of such intensity and changes of pace and command that it was astonishing that Verdasco appeared to have played its entirety without a hair or a shirt crease out of place.

In the aftermath of Murray's success, seeking out Sir Alex for a quick word was not that difficult; we had chatted at length in the middle of the football season about the US Open final, which he had attended as a guest of the Murray family, and it was clear he was getting the tennis bug. "Would you be back for the final [should Andy be in it]?" I asked. But Sir Alex had long planned a celebratory retirement cruise with his family and closest friends around the Scottish isles and thought he would be somewhere in the vicinity of Tobermory, on the Isle of Mull, when the men's denouement was scheduled. He said he would be tuning in, though.

For him, watching tennis was far more mentally draining than pinpointing the fortunes of his former team Manchester United, for at least there he could enjoy the release of leaping from his seat, dashing to the side of the pitch and letting out his emotions. You cannot do that when you are seated a row behind the Duke of Kent.

Paul Hayward, the sports writer of the year, was on the ball as ever in the *Daily Telegraph*: "There were times when you felt Sir Alex Ferguson would be more use as [Murray's] manager than his supporter, to rid him of his faintly apologetic air on Centre Court. Reading reviews of Murray's comeback against Verdasco there was still a whiff of accusation: that he nearly messed it up, that he should never have been in that position in the first place (despite facing a lefty for the first time this year), and that he is still only one big sulk away from disaster. Others pointed out that two years ago he would have lost to Verdasco. The theatricality remains, but the difference is that Murray now expects to win that kind of match, while in the past he only aspired to."

Verdasco came within a few games of sealing a place in his first Wimbledon semi-final

Each of the men's quarter-finals, as we might have expected, contained enough emotion to require four or five changes of shirt – just for the spectators. On Centre Court, the sensations began in the first game of the match between Juan Martin Del Potro and David Ferrer as the Argentine, lulled into playing a backhand to a ball that stopped on him, went careering over behind the baseline, hyper-extending the knee that had been tightly bound by bandages from the first exchanges of The Championships.

"I was close to retiring," Del Potro said. "I was worried because it felt just like what happened five days ago. The doctor said they can't do any more with my knee. I had the tape, a very tight tape, and that helped me to move a little bit, but nothing more." There was something more, however. The doctor, who had been summoned to join the physiotherapist and officials, prescribed nothing more complicated than two Paracetamol tablets. "Some magic pills," a delighted Del Potro said later.

After the fall, he had resumed gingerly, as you would have expected, following a break of seven minutes. It took a while but, even before the first set had been settled, Del Potro had acquired sufficient movement to accompany his big serving and trademark hammer forehand. Ferrer, one of the best returners in tennis, could not cope with the Del Potro serve. The Spaniard, who had reached his first Grand Slam singles final at the 2013 French Open, managed just one break point and a single deuce in Del Potro's 15 service games. Few can cope with the forehand that was so prominent in Del Potro's 2009 US Open success.

Juan Martin Del Potro **(left)** *withstood an early tumble on his already-injured knee to see off the battling exploits of David Ferrer* **(below)**

Tennis has been waiting for the 'Tower of Tandil' to be able to train and stay free from injury long enough for him to re-join the elite. The match concluded, in a 6-2, 6-4, 7-6(5) victory, with two points that will remain in the mind's eye for some time – a forehand cross-court riposte to one just as startling from Ferrer and, the last knockings, a rally of pure instinct and crisp hitting, each shot more stunning than its predecessor, until Del Potro, dragged out wide, hammered a forehand across the high part of the net. He lay on his back, arms thrust into the air, cherishing his moment of triumph.

On No.1 Court at the time, Tomas Berdych looked as if he might do something that would send yet another shockwave across the portals of the Club, as if there had not been enough of those in the previous eight days of competition. He looked as if he might take a set from the world No.1. A stunned air of almost sickly disbelief gripped the court and its environs. "Grown men and women clutched their faces, pulled their children closer to them and looked on aghast, unable to measure the full impact of what seemed to be unfolding in front of them," wrote Giles Smith in *The Times*.

Berdych didn't manage to achieve what he had been threatening, though. Leading 3-0 in the second set was by no means as definitive an insurance policy as he might have felt it would be, his confidence boosted by Djokovic's body language which was as downbeat as it had been at any time in the event. The Czech player, though, couldn't capitalise. It was as if he himself froze and soon enough he had won a single game in seven and the tide had inexorably turned against him. Djokovic would seize a 7-6(5), 6-4, 6-3 victory and a place against Del Potro in the last four.

17 The number of five-set matches at The Championships 2013, out of 124 completed, the lowest percentage of five-setters at Wimbledon since 1968.

Back to Murray. His somewhat less than fruity tennis in the first two sets against an inspired Verdasco was followed by some rather more fruity language of self-admonishment as he sat down and contemplated how he might pull himself out of the mess. Verdasco looked impregnable, swinging through his forehand, swinging through his serve, crunching everything within range, confidence infused by a new Babolat racket, the kind with which Rafael Nadal has tormented opponents for a long time. But, as is his wont, Murray refused to buckle. He rallied to win the third set 6-1 and the fourth 6-4. Although he tried to appear confident in the Royal Box (at one stage leaning nonchalantly with his arm across the back of his chair), Ferguson was soon bolt upright, for the fifth set would either demoralise or delight.

For British purposes, it delighted. Murray was 3-4, 15-30 down when Verdasco manoeuvred himself into a position to play a backhand down the line, the likes of which he had plundered all afternoon, but at the last second he chose to go cross-court. That was it, there and then. Murray held and then broke Verdasco in the 11th game, forcing a forehand error with a defiant forehand of his own. The last service game was easy-peasy. "I didn't rush when I went two sets down," Murray said. "The more matches you play, the more you learn to appreciate how to turn matches around and to change the momentum."

Simultaneously on No.1 Court, the battle of the Poles was being fought out and to the favour of young Jerzy Janowicz who defeated Lukasz Kubot 7-5, 6-4, 6-4. The match ended with the pair in an embrace, and exchanging shirts in the middle of the court, before Janowicz collapsed, elated and utterly filled, into his chair. He was sobbing so much that Kubot had to tap him on the shoulder and remind him when it was time to leave the premises. Murray v Janowicz to come. The mind boggled.

Novak Djokovic **(below)** *was surprisingly untested by Tomas Berdych* **(below right)**

Jerzy Janowicz **(top and bottom)** *and Lukasz Kubot* **(middle)** *made history as they became the first Poles ever to compete against each other in a Grand Slam singles match*

DAY TEN
THURSDAY 4 JULY

The second Thursday of The Championships, when a British player is preparing for the next day's men's semi-finals, tends to be perhaps the most hectic day for a British writer. Only if there was a British player in the ladies' semi-finals would the focus be 100 per cent on the tennis being played that day but, inevitably, one's thoughts were a little addled.

"I saw the ball like a football," Marion Bartoli said

You wanted to devote full attention to the ladies on court, for they wholly merited it, at the same time as not missing a trick where the men's preparation was concerned, so a couple of trips to the practice courts before play were essential: a little look at how Jerzy Janowicz was serving (like a steam train at speed), and a sense of Andy Murray's manner (very decent in the circumstances). Janowicz then did a trawl of the television studios, almost stopping between pop-up appearances to speak to myself and S.L. Price of *Sports Illustrated*. These interviews on the hoof were alarming because Janowicz is such a tall man that you couldn't quite see the expression on his face as he was speaking and you were walking alongside him. Nevertheless, we learned that he had been an aficionado of Pete Sampras – the seven-time Wimbledon champion – growing up. "It is hard to explain when you love someone," he said, "but it was the style of Sampras, what he brought to the court, his unbelievable serve and his beautiful, beautiful slice also."

Leaving Janowicz to dream Sampras dreams, it was time to take to the Centre Court, and a first semi-final that did not really extend long enough to leave a lasting impression. Marion Bartoli woke up from a nap in the locker room half an hour before the match; Kirsten Flipkens must have wished she had stayed asleep. Sadly for Flipkens, the occasion of a debut at this stratum of the sport hit her like a tsunami. She did not look relaxed from the outset, her timing was awry and she did not react as she should.

Before she had taken her nap, Bartoli was captured on film by Jonas Bjorkman, the former men's singles semi-finalist and now a TV commentator in Sweden, hitting forehand after forehand without pause as balls were tossed to her with barely a second's interval between them. She seemed to middle each and every one and the same principle followed when she took to the court, pounding shots at Flipkens whose defences, so noted in earlier matches, simply crumbled away.

If Bartoli is in a mean ball-striking mood, if her movement is good, if she believes entirely, then she takes some stopping. On this early afternoon, with the threat of a shower in the region, her play was brutal and unrelenting. She allowed her opponent only two points in the first three games of the second set, at which point Flipkens called for the trainer for a knee injury. "Marion played an amazing match," Flipkens said. "But I fell in the first set. At that moment I didn't feel it, but a couple of games later I started to feel a really sharp pain. I tried my slices. She didn't have any problem with that. I tried the drop shot. She got it. I tried to come to the net and she lobbed me. I tried everything, actually." But Bartoli matched and mastered all that was thrown at her. At the end, having breezed through 6-1, 6-2, she contorted herself into a shape that would not have looked out of place at your local yoga class. And then, quite probably, she went back to sleep.

"I needed a nap to recover from my early morning practice, so it was just a quick 15, 20 minutes," she said. "It was in the ladies' dressing room. I am French. Corsican. I know I am crazy. I said to Vic, the

Kirsten Flipkens **(above)** *could do little against the pace and precision of Bartoli* **(below left)***, who dropped just three games*

physio upstairs, to wake me up just in case, but I actually woke up myself at 12.30. Then I went for a warm-up. That's just the way I am."

If either Sabine Lisicki or Agnieszka Radwanska had been thinking of a long spell in the locker room before their second semi-final, such notions were dashed by the ease of Bartoli's passage to the final. And if the first semi-final had been a little less than dramatic – save for Bartoli's leaping preparatory swishes at thin air at which linesmen and ball boys and girls often ducked and weaved out of the way – the second became one of the matches of the tournament, one of wildly fluctuating play.

As Simon Barnes in *The Times* said: "Lisicki's tactic is to get into a position from which victory is logically impossible. Once she gets there, she finds the resources to win. It's not something you would recommend to everyone, but it works for her. Faced with devastation at the hands of the brilliant, cerebral tennis of Radwanska, she crumbled like a digestive biscuit and then miraculously uncrumbled herself and won. She won 6-4, 2-6, 9-7 in a match of rare and glorious beauty."

If you recall, Lisicki had lost nine games in succession before turning the tables on Serena Williams, losing the second set 6-1 and being 3-0 down in the decider. It was then that she found herself. After shading a tight (and brilliant) first set, Lisicki made an ungodly mess of the second, aided, it has to be said, by the guile and accuracy of her opponent. Radwanska plays with such intelligence that they ought to scrub out the tennis court markings and paint the lawn with 64 black-and-white squares. Lisicki dropped five service games in succession and was 3-0 down again. From a hopeless situation, she found hope. "I remembered what I had done against Serena and that gave me so much hope," she said. A power surge and the German drew level, and then forced her way ahead, breaking the Polish serve once more and ready to serve for a place in the final at 5-4. Radwanska broke back easily, however, with a focused, crafty game, but she just couldn't find a way to break Lisicki's booming serve down the stretch.

With a second chance to serve for the match, Lisicki made no mistakes, firing home a forehand winner on match point and collapsing to the ground in tears. To say that the handshake between the pair was terse would be an understatement. But there was nothing to dent the joy in the 23-year-old becoming the first German to reach a Wimbledon singles final since seven-time champion Steffi Graf in 1999. Lisicki v Bartoli would not have been the final many would have chosen before The Championships but, from the deluge, it looked hugely appropriate.

There were no Americans left in the main draw of the singles but in the boys' event they found a reason to be cheerful. I stopped by for a few minutes to take in a few games of the quarter-final between Kyle Edmund of Great Britain and 15-year-old Stefan Kozlov of the USA, via Macedonia. There was something about Kozlov that immediately took the eye, a distinctive style, a throwback haircut, a face that reminded me of the Belarusian Vladimir Voltchkov, a semi-finalist here in 2000, and a game that, if it did not have tremendous power as yet, was splendid in every other regard. The Americans may have unearthed – or should that be imported – a rough diamond which, in the right hands, could be polished to distinct achievement. Watch out for this kid.

Few other Brits were taking notice; they were too busy keeping tabs on Mr Murray and his entourage. Tim Henman, now of the BBC, suggested that the 2012 men's final between Murray and Roger Federer was the most intensely pressurised match he had ever witnessed and that nothing else would come close to beating it in those terms. "He [Murray] will never feel such pressure again," Henman remarked. He also said that when he commentated on Murray he "would quite like to open the door and shout over the top of the canvas". What pieces of advice would he offer? "I'm not sure it would be too technical," Henman replied. "I had my moments when I wasn't playing well. I got into some pretty deep holes but I'd like to think there was a slightly clear picture of what I was trying to do."

WIMBLEDON IN NUMBERS

1999
The last time a German player featured in a Wimbledon singles final, when Steffi Graf lost to Lindsay Davenport.

(Far left) *Agnieszka Radwanska was bidding to reach her second consecutive Wimbledon final*

(Below) *But she was undone by a fightback of epic proportions from Sabine Lisicki*

The unbeatable Bryans

While the eyes of the Wimbledon-watching public were firmly planted on Andy Murray's quest for history, or Novak Djokovic's attempt to achieve further Grand Slam success, two brothers were setting about making some more history of their own. Bob and Mike Bryan, the Olympic, US Open, Australian Open and French Open champions were aiming to become the first pair ever to hold all four majors and Olympic gold at the same time. And with their nail-biting five-set finish over Rohan Bopanna and Edouard Roger-Vasselin on Day Ten, winning 6-7(4), 6-4, 6-3, 5-7, 6-3, the twins were one step away.

"It would probably be the highest achievement. It doesn't happen every day. I mean, it would be really cool, I mean, to say that we've had a couple records. To add this on top would just be really sweet," Mike said.

"These type of records and achievements, there's a lot of them. They're always out there. You know, this one's extra cool. There will always be something else to do."

Winning Wimbledon would not only be their 91st ATP title together; just for good measure, the Bryans are also the only pair to win all nine ATP Masters Series 1000 events too.

DAY ELEVEN
FRIDAY 5 JULY

T here were several different connotations on the same contentious theme on Day Eleven, to do with the words 'raising' and 'roof'. Except that is from the gloriously weather-obsessed *Daily Express*, which informed us that Britain was about to be struck by a deadly heatwave.

Novak Djokovic was at his springiest as he played the match of the tournament to beat Juan Martin Del Potro and advance to his second Wimbledon final

The roof in question was our old friend of the Centre Court variety, and the man who was raising it was Andy Murray. The Scot led Jerzy Janowicz by two sets to one in the second men's singles semi-final which had been a bit of a set-to thus far. Murray lost the first set on a tie-break, won the second with varying degrees of difficulty and also the third from 4-1 down, having secured two breaks and with his opponent rocking a little bit. Janowicz had been spluttering on about the roof for a couple of changeovers. It was just past 8.40pm.

It was at this point that Murray, about as buoyant as he had been all day, received a tap on the shoulder which he would have preferred not to receive. Referee Andrew Jarrett's first on-court visitation was to inform the two players that he was going to operate the machinery. Janowicz allowed himself a Bond villain-type smile, as Murray did not so much talk about the roof, but hit it.

"It's ridiculous, it's not even dark. You can't close it now. This is an outdoor tournament. I don't understand these rules." There was no going back on the decision, though, and when he had had time to cool down, talk to his team, get his game head back on and stride out under cover, it was to complete a four-set victory, 6-7(2), 6-4, 6-4, 6-3, of real substance. He was into a second consecutive Wimbledon final, where he would face the world No.1, Novak Djokovic.

A men's event that had been littered with tales of the unexpected reached the conclusion which the seedings demanded after two very different matches, the first of which was to be so thoroughly brilliant as to merit a place among the best ever seen at The Championships. For that, the departure of Argentina's Juan Martin Del Potro from SW19 was both a sadness and an abiding memory of grace and goodly hitting.

"In an age of Twitter and text messages, of instant gratification and endangered attention spans, men's tennis continues – despite all the ferocious currents to the contrary – to excel at long form," wrote Christoper Clarey in the *New York Times*. "The marathon men were at it again [on] Friday, this time on Centre Court at Wimbledon in the sunlight, where yet another set of powerful, evenly matched rivals relentlessly and good-naturedly sent each other scrambling, lunging, sprawling to every straight line and corner of the most famous patch of grass in the game." Clarey had nailed it with word-perfect clarity.

"I think this match is going to be a memory for a few years," Del Potro said. "We play for four hours and a half on a very high level. We didn't make too many errors. I don't know if the rest of the players can play like us today." The No.8 seed, back in a Grand Slam semi-final for the first time since winning the 2009 US Open, saved two match points in the fourth-set tie-break, winning the final four points to take it 8-6. The crowd was in a real tizzy. Shortly after, the match hit the four-hour mark, surpassing the 1989 match between Boris Becker and Ivan Lendl as the longest match at this stage in the long history of The Championships.

There had been fears that Del Potro would not be physically fit enough to go toe to toe with Djokovic but – despite taking a breather during this line-call challenge – he was, pushing the world No.1 through five thrilling sets

(Previous pages)
It was a display of the type of physical endurance that has come to epitomise the highest order of men's tennis

Andy Murray **(right)** *had to account for the firepower of young Pole Jerzy Janowicz* **(below)**, *but produced an accomplished performance*

It was indeed, a match for the ages, played at such a high intensity and with breakneck hitting from both men. I seemed to be writing the words 'stunning rally' at the end of every point, my notebook was littered with circles (around those points that require special mention), with break point chances and moves of exception. In the final set, Del Potro had break points first but the Djokovic backhand – that shot of such immense reliability – saved the day. In the next game, the Serbian extended himself to a break point but netted a forehand. The crunch eventually came in the eighth game when the Del Potro forehand, a shot with which he has scored so much success across the world, finally came unglued. He covered his eyes at the miss but recovered enough to secure a break point when the Serb served for the match, only for Djokovic to be able to fashion a backhand winner, having been helped by a net-cord during the rally. Djokovic then thumped home another cleanly-struck backhand for a 7-5, 4-6, 7-6(2), 6-7(6), 6-3 success and the two men fell into an embrace.

I had been pondering a compilation of the greatest best-of-five-set matches in The Championships' history. There was the 2008 final between Rafael Nadal and Roger Federer with its amazing conclusion, the 1977 semi-final between Bjorn Borg and Vitas Gerulaitis, and my personal favourite – the 1983 semi-final between Chris Lewis of New Zealand and South African Kevin Curren that rendered its victor, Lewis, unable to win more than six games in the final against John McEnroe. This latest encounter deserved to rank among those greats.

How Djokovic would pitch up on Sunday we would soon discover. He departed to leave the stage for Murray and Janowicz. Much would rest on how the Pole acclimatised to his first taste of such an occasion. Coming into the match, he had figured prominently in two statistical lists: top of the aces, with 94, and second in double faults, with 26. He would add to both and would not flinch from trusting his best weapon, sending down his serves at more than 140 miles per hour (139mph in his first service game) from above the chair umpire's eye-line.

Trailing 4-5 and two set points down after just over half an hour, Janowicz held with two huge second serves, signalling that he was not overawed by the event, the setting or the opponent. He gave Murray more than the odd hard look as he let his daggers fly to force a tie-break, a place where one would imagine a server of his strength would be most comfortable, even though in 2013 he had won 11 of them and lost 10. Murray's count was 14-5 but, having gone 4-0 down after a shocker of a volley, he double-faulted to surrender the set.

Janowicz was hugely encouraged now to imagine he could shock the tennis world but, when Murray drove a volley at him, Lendl-like, in the first game of the second set (and it stayed in), the Pole spun out of the way and simmered – then served two double faults to drop serve. With the help of his third ace, Janowicz saved two break points to hold in the fifth game but blew two on Murray's serve. "Frustration followed impatience, breeding looseness," wrote Kevin Mitchell in *The Guardian*.

Janowicz had three break points in the eighth game, but could not crack the Murray wall, though it was beginning to look a bit crumbly around the edges. He played the drop shot incredibly well, too, a tactic that constantly forced Murray, as he raced forward, to make decent upwards tracks. But his good

The semi-final was interrupted at the end of the third set as the Centre Court roof was closed for light

Murray's grit and determination was evident as he reached his second Wimbledon final, to the delight of Ross Hutchins **(right)** *and the rest of Murray's team*

WIMBLEDON IN NUMBERS

4hrs 43mins

The match time between Djokovic and Del Potro, the longest men's semi-final in Wimbledon history, outlasting Boris Becker and Ivan Lendl's 4hrs 1min effort in 1989.

form aside, Janowicz was getting anxious about the light. At 4-5, the 22-year-old asked the chair umpire, Jake Garner, why the under-eaves lights were coming on. Murray, who had seen it all before, served out the set to level, unperturbed and relaxed. As Murray took a comfort break, Janowicz again asked about the greying skies and if the roof would be drawn across. No, he was told, there was at least an hour's natural light left. It was just before 8pm.

Then Murray, having hauled himself back to win that third set, thinking he had his man on the ropes, was told he would have to wait 20 minutes to attempt to soften him up once more. Janowicz's argument had swayed the referee. Murray, shocked, needed to regroup and was a little astounded to find Janowicz on his mobile phone in the locker room during the hiatus as the roof was closed and the airflow system kicked in. "My God," he said to himself, "he's relaxed." But Murray was, too. And when he is relaxed, he can play devilishly good tennis.

I described it in *The Times* as "a wonderful, heart-warming, emotion-sapping, generous, glorious, stupendous Friday". I don't take a word of it back.

The Centre Court crowd rose to salute Murray's achievements under the roof as the world No.2 celebrated in his customary fashion

DAY TWELVE
SATURDAY 6 JULY

I t was less than an hour before the ladies' singles final, a time when you would expect the protagonists to be deep in their pre-match routines and yet there, on the players' lawn, was Marion Bartoli, happily engaging with her group, laughing and boisterous, as if she didn't have a worry in the world.

Chair Umpire Eva Asderaki, Marion Bartoli, Sabine Lisicki and Referee Andrew Jarrett pose with 14-year-old Sophie Snowling for the coin toss. Sophie represented East Anglia's Children's Hospices who are supporting her brother Jake

For all one knew, Sabine Lisicki may have been just as relaxed. She had certainly given that impression the previous day, her toothy smile forever evident, as she charmed a succession of interviewers. If she could bring such a relaxed air of contentment to the final, she would be very difficult to beat, especially given the quality of players (Samantha Stosur, Serena Williams and Agnieszka Radwanska, to name but three) against whom she had previously shown such courage.

But the final day is different. The sensations are peculiar. The air may be sweeter but it can sometimes be a sweet sickliness as if something is not quite normal. When a bouquet of flowers was presented to Lisicki as she prepared to walk onto Centre Court for her first Grand Slam singles final experience, she looked at them, looked ahead, and sensed a new, rather uneasy pressure.

Bartoli, by comparison, was jaunty. She smiled. She felt good. Her father Walter had arrived from France the previous evening and they had left the Grounds on Friday arm in arm, as they had been so many times during her career when it seemed like Dad and daughter were against everyone else. And yet, in the past few months, they had attempted a separation (in purely tennis terms), come back together and then parted again. Walter – who had foregone his career in pharmaceuticals to teach his daughter tennis – completely trusted in Marion's instincts and was content that in the company of Amelie Mauresmo, the 2006 Wimbledon champion and French Fed Cup captain, her new hitting partner Thomas Drouet and her trainers, she was more than equipped to win.

But for the final, he could not stay away nor did she want him to. Remarkably, it was on these Grounds two years ago that she had asked him to leave the side of the court because of the intensity of his presence – after the first set of what would prove to be a three-hour, three-set, third round meeting with Flavia Pennetta of Italy. Marion had turned and airily dismissed Walter and his wife Sophie, telling them to watch the match from somewhere else. "I needed to express something somehow," she said at the time. "I needed the frustration to get out. I could have smashed a racket. I just needed to do something to release the frustration and start again. I normally never act like that."

During The Championships, Drouet spoke with Walter several times, nothing too technical, just the odd comment and reassuring assessment. There was no doubt he would be back. "It is very important for me," Marion said. "My dad is associated with everything. It is super important to share this between a daughter and her father. It wouldn't be normal in a way if he wasn't here."

Lisicki, too, had her father in the box. Richard Lisicki was the paramount coach, although the family had recently brought Wim Fissette, who had been instrumental in coaching Kim Clijsters during her comeback, into the team. As a company, they had done extremely well. All was set.

From start to finish, Bartoli (above) gave Lisicki (below) no quarter in a largely lopsided final

It was a day of just rewards for Marion Bartoli, runner-up at Wimbledon in 2007, who produced an emphatic performance to claim the Grand Slam title she said she "knew she had always been capable of winning". Serving an ace on match point, Bartoli ran across the court (below left) *and climbed up into the players' box to celebrate with her team. Posing with the Venus Rosewater Dish* (below) *alongside her opponent, she proved a very popular champion*

The start would be crucial. When Lisicki hit a backhand winner to secure a first break point – saved by a thumping two-handed forehand via a net-cord – then Bartoli tossed in a double fault to offer another break chance, which was conceded with a second consecutive double, there was a feeling that nerves may have been a French preserve. Not so. Lisicki promptly double-faulted the advantage away, a point emphasised when Bartoli produced her first ace on game point to lead 2-1.

Sadly for the German, this was to be the prelude to a run of collecting only a single game from 11 (and she saved four break points in that one as well) during which her hopes disappeared in a puff of dust from the Centre Court baseline. Such was the sense of woe that overcame her that Lisicki spent the latter half of the match fighting back tears as she tried to put her serve into the court – she won just 52 per cent of her first-serve points – while Bartoli was the epitome of focus, intensity and calm.

The crowd wanted to come on and give Lisicki a communal hug. She was distraught, it was difficult to serve through the tears. She tried to smile but in truth the occasion had overcome her as it had others in the past. The more she threw the ball up to serve, the less her toss went in the right direction, and she could barely lift her legs from the baseline. There were two more double faults in the fifth game of the second set. Had she won that to bring the score to 3-2, German hopes may have been elevated.

Ladies' singles champion Marion Bartoli greets the crowds from the Centre Court Members' Balcony

In the seventh game, championship points down, Lisicki fired a brave backhand drive volley into court, produced a service winner on the next, then drew a backhand error from Bartoli, and held on to survive what would have been the worst mauling in a ladies' final since 1975, when Billie Jean King defeated Evonne Goolagong Cawley for the loss of a single game in 38 minutes. Instead, Lisicki broke in the next game for 5-3 and held for 5-4.

Brilliant Bartoli

How much do you think winning Wimbledon will change your life?

"It will not change me as a person because I will always remain the same: very humble, very low-key and easygoing, down-to-earth. But just hearing 'Wimbledon champion', that kind of sounds good to me. It has been my dream. I wanted that so badly. I felt the achievement of my career was to win a Grand Slam. I kept dreaming. I kept my head up. I kept working hard, and it just happened."

So many setbacks, yet you've prevailed. Is there a certain strength in that?

"I'm a very tough person. I can focus and be really as strong as wood. I think it's coming from my childhood, from where I practised when I was younger, from those very tough situations. I needed to handle going to school, normally practising at 10pm, finishing at midnight, going back to school the next day. Those kind of hard moments make me extremely strong when I'm on the tennis court."

Does it make it extra special for you that you're different from the rest?

"I believe to be a Grand Slam champion you have to be a bit different. You have to be strong in your mind and your opinion. I felt I received a tremendous amount of support. When I was on the court, you could see people clapping me at the end of the match. I think you can feel all the respect. Even if I'm not maybe playing the same style of game, I think the attitude I'm carrying on the court, the mental strength and everything, it's maybe something they can look at."

There was jubilation for the Bryan brothers **(above and right)**, who claimed the men's doubles title in four sets to hold all four Grand Slams at once, while Hsieh Su-Wei and Peng Shuai **(far right)** lifted the ladies' doubles trophies

But that was where the spirit and the shot-making of Bartoli became supreme again – a crisp service game, a conclusive hold completed with an ace of all things and she was a Grand Slam champion, a Wimbledon champion, 6-1, 6-4, the first Frenchwoman to win the title since her close friend Mauresmo seven years earlier. In doing so she became the first woman in the Open era to win Wimbledon without facing a top 10 seed and only the sixth to win such a title without dropping a set.

"I think I was just overwhelmed by this whole situation," Lisicki said on court. "Credit to Marion. She's been in that situation before and she handled it so well. I hope I'll get the chance one more time as well, I want to thank my entire team for being there for me. We've been through so much, through ups and downs, and this was my first slam final and I wish I won it. But I hope we get there one more time."

Bartoli, her eyes glinting, spoke with great elegance and charm. "I know how it feels Sabine, and I'm *sure* you will be here one more time, no doubt about it. I've been practising my serve for so long, at least I saved it for the best moment. First of all, I want to thank my dad who is here with me today. It means so much." And then she reminded the audience that she had begun her Wimbledon campaign on Court 14; it was remarkable what went through people's heads at these moments.

Bob and Mike Bryan have spent a lifetime knowing what the other was thinking. The twins came into the men's doubles final having won the last three Grand Slam titles and the Olympic gold medal for the United States on this court the previous August. Could they become the first team in the Open era to hold all five accolades at the same time? Well, for a few minutes, it seemed as though Croatia's Ivan Dodig and Marcelo Melo of Brazil, the No.12 seeds, might upset the apple cart.

Melo and Dodig looked unbeatable in the opening phase and the brothers found themselves 4-0 down within 11 minutes, with their opponents going on to clinch the set 6-3. Mike Bryan, in particular, looked shell-shocked and far from his usual clinical self at the net. But the 35-year-old brothers slowly worked it out, their long experience telling as their trademark heavy serves and quick-fire volleys made inroads into their talented but callow opponents. At their best they move almost as a single entity connected by elastic – 'Bryan Bryan'. In the end, they triumphed 3-6, 6-3, 6-4, 6-4 to clinch the so-called 'Golden Bryan Slam' in their 25th Grand Slam final.

The ladies' doubles title was won by the No.8 seeds, Hsieh Su-Wei of Chinese Taipei (coached by the two-time former Wimbledon doubles champion Paul McNamee) and Peng Shuai of China, who defeated the Australians Ashleigh Barty and Casey Dellacqua 7-6(1), 6-1.

Italy's Gianluigi Quinzi (top) *triumphed in the boys' singles while Belinda Bencic* (above), *coached by Martina Hingis's mother Melanie Molitor, won the girls' singles*

WIMBLEDON IN NUMBERS

6 The number of Ladies' Singles champions at Wimbledon to win the title without dropping a set, after Marion Bartoli joined that group.

DAY THIRTEEN

SUNDAY 7 JULY

It could not have been a nicer day had it tried. A year ago, the forecast was not portentous; they said rain and by golly did it rain, overhead and on the court. Those tears, those grievous tears. Did we have to see them again? They showed us anyway. Now, an amiable forecaster was telling us to pack sunscreen and not to forget a hat. And drink plenty of fluids. A perfect July day awaited, just the day to celebrate a perfect story.

World No. 1 Novak Djokovic and world No. 2 Andy Murray stride onto Centre Court for the final, watched by Gerard Butler, Wayne Rooney (top right) *and David Cameron* (bottom right) *in the Royal Box*

Everywhere you turned, every station you listened – or contributed – to, appeared to have Andy Murray pegged for a win. I said so on *Sportsweek*, having said so the previous night in a BBC radio debate mentioning that I'd walked past Fred Perry's statue that afternoon and wished the great man, someone I had come to know in his latter years, a peaceful night's rest and much peace thereafter. There was no going back on such pronouncements.

Andy Murray was better equipped in 2013 than the previous year – there was no getting away from that fact. He had won the US Open in 2012 to break his Grand Slam duck, he had won the Olympic gold medal on Centre Court, he had tightened up specific areas of his game, he was in beastly physical shape, he had survived his silly matches in The Championships, and he had in his sights a player whose form and ranking made this the pure achievement – to win Wimbledon, taking down the No. 1 player in the world to do so.

A smiling start

Novak Djokovic had said his grass game had never been better, he had survived brutal challenges from Tomas Berdych and Juan Martin Del Potro in previous rounds, and looked in stunning shape. This was a final fit to be played before an arrayed audience and it was no surprise that the President of Serbia was there, as was the British Prime Minister, the Leader of the Opposition and the First Minister of Scotland, who had something blue and white and which fluttered tucked away just in case.

There were a sprinkling of top-rate sports people around too: Wayne Rooney, the England footballer, and Justin Rose, who had won the US Open golf title three weeks earlier, were in the posh seats; Sir Chris Hoy – Murray's fellow Scot – had taken up a more discreet pew amid his support team a couple of seats away from Will, Andy's father.

"Novak pats Andy on the back before the off," I tweeted. "Then both go to the wrong side." "What a first point, where's my water supply?" was my second of 53 despatched during the match. The early exchanges of the final were of a fashion that suggested we had better settle in for the long haul. They were hard-fought, both players flighting, slicing, dipping and crushing their shots. Murray had trouble with his right shoe and fiddled with it but broke to lead 2-1 on his fourth chance and then played sloppily to gift the break back. In the sixth game he held to love, then broke to love to lead 4-3 before double-faulting the first two points of the eighth game. Murray saved the first break point with an ace. He staved off the second with a forehand volley winner at the end of a rally which continued even after Mohamed Lahyani, the umpire, had seemed to call a baseline ball long (overruling a lineswoman). A third was denied Djokovic with a forehand that completely bamboozled him and Murray held for 5-3 when his opponent netted a forehand. Two games later, the first set would be his, courtesy of an ace and two service winners.

There was a suggestion that something might be awry with Djokovic's wrist in the early stages of the second set but otherwise he was settled enough to break serve in the fourth game. Although he stumbled a couple of times on the dusty patches behind the baseline, he held to lead 4-1. Murray had been adrift by the same score to Jerzy Janowicz in the third set of the semi-final and came back to win it. His response here was similar although, in the seventh game, he wasted chances to take advantage of screwed first serves and was grateful when Djokovic double-faulted the game away.

The coin toss for the men's singles final was performed by 11-year-old Pinki Sonkar, representing Smile Train, the world's leading cleft surgery charity for children. Smile Train is one of the charities supported by the Wimbledon Foundation from the proceeds of the ticket resale scheme at The Championships in 2013 (which, with a matching contribution from HSBC, the official banking partner to The Championships, raised over £300,000 for charity). The Wimbledon Foundation has recently been established to co-ordinate and enhance the wide-ranging programme of community, charitable and development activities of the All England Club and The Championships. Pinki certainly gave a joyful smile.

WIMBLEDON
FOUNDATION

Come on Andy!

The queue to sit on Murray Mound during the men's singles final had begun on Saturday evening, as spectators flocked from far and wide to share in Murray's moment. Fans from Scotland (*above*, *below*, and *right*) were there in great numbers, while Wimbledon visitors also watched from No.2 Court (*below right*). The decibel level on the Mound as Murray sealed his victory was as loud as a rock concert.

Of the many pivotal games in the match, the eighth of the second set was momentous. From 30-0 on the Murray serve, Djokovic rallied to secure a break point. Murray steadied over the next delivery, sent it thundering out wide, Djokovic challenged the call of 'good' and Hawk-Eye showed that it had brushed the line. Murray's jaw was clenched, as was his fist. Then the British challenger had to save another, this time with an adroit overhead after taking command of the rally. He played a delicious backhand drop shot to move to game point and won it with a serve that clipped the centre line and to which Djokovic could not fashion a return. 4-4.

Djokovic held, without blinking, to love; Murray a little more hesitantly to 30. At 5-5, the Serb was 15-40 down and held steady beneath an overhead to fight off one break point but subsequently played a tired-looking forehand. Murray's 6-5 advantage became a two-set lead when he served out to love, completing the deal with another thumping ace. The last man to come from two sets down to win the Wimbledon final was Henri Cochet of France in 1927 and Murray had no desire to join Jean Borotra in that list.

The third set started in just the manner that an increasingly hot and bothered Centre Court crowd had wished, as Djokovic lost serve when his own backhand slice, which had floated long, was called in before Murray's challenge was upheld. Behind that break, he served out to love. Djokovic was 0-2, 0-30 down. The murmuring intensified. Was he going to fold? Not on your nelly. He held on and broke Murray in the fourth game when a backhand volley was nudged wide. Not only that, Murray's next service game was also plundered, rather too quickly for local tastes. Djokovic had won four games in

Murray was as comfortable on Centre Court as he has ever been

a row, a potentially decisive changing of the order. His drop shot was beginning to wound yet, as the legendary Australian coach Harry Hopman once said, "the drop shot is usually a sign of tiredness", and Djokovic, although ahead, was taking very deep breaths.

The Serbian had to hold but he could not, Murray scoring on his second break opportunity when Djokovic erred on the backhand. The four games in a row for Djokovic became three for Murray when he used his forehand more aggressively, bossing the points, stepping in, sticking out his chin. His performance to break in the ninth was the most awesome. A running forehand that earned the second of his opportunities brought to mind my visit to his training camp in Miami the previous December and all those straining, gutsy, up-court dashes accompanied by the urgings of Jez Green, his trainer, to make it and make it again. The Prime Minister was on his feet and there were no questions for him to answer. Steady on, Mr Cameron. Djokovic flailed at a forehand. Murray would serve for the championship. Centre Court was on the verge of going completely bonkers.

"Good God, what must the man have been going through?" Martin Samuel of the *Daily Mail* wondered. There are 90 seconds at a changeover, enough time to let your mind wander, enough time to consider the prospects of holding or not holding, of letting imaginings run riot. There did not seem anything wrong with Murray's stride as he walked back to the roller end to serve. In no time at all he led 40-0, the second point concluding with another surge of pace to close on the net and flick away a forehand winner. This is where the notebook became a little blurry, the handwriting a touch wobbly.

Meanwhile Djokovic struggled to interrupt Murray's momentum

The moment of truth

After Murray saw three match points come and go, on the fourth, Djokovic's backhand found the net. Murray's racket slipped from his grasp, and he turned towards the Centre Court crowd in disbelief. Having wandered around in a daze before falling to the ground, he later said that serving out that game was one of the most challenging moments of his professional career.

Historic final between Roger Federer and Andy Murray began in the sunshine on

5.27 ♛ ROLEX ♛

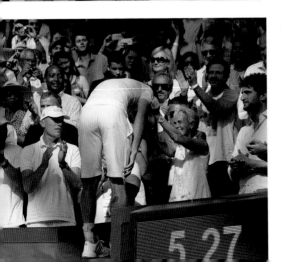

Having been congratulated by Djokovic **(far left)**, Murray lifted his arms in celebration before falling to the ground as the sheer weight of his achievement began to hit home. While his name was being inscribed onto the Challenge Cup by engraver Roman Zoltowski **(left)**, Murray crossed the court to celebrate with his team, including girlfriend Kim and his mother Judy

Djokovic saved the first championship point with a feathery forehand volley after a nerve-racking rally; the second when he thumped away a half-court second serve; the third when Murray missed a backhand. Then the Serb had a break point but missed a forehand service return. "Come on," Murray retorted. A second break point (gained by an extraordinary net-cord when Djokovic soft-handed a half-volley, the ball clipping the top of the net and dying) was rescued when Murray clinched another heart-in-mouth rally with a flicked forehand. A third, brilliantly brought about when Djokovic flicked a forehand winner from a drop shot, was denied by a lovely backhand volley after Murray had opened up the court with a crunching forehand.

The next point would be one of the most brilliant Murray had played – attacking forehand, rolled forehand, sliced backhand, defensive backhand lob, thunderous backhand riposte to an overhead, and a forward burst to breach the world No.1's defences. A fourth championship point. Murray served, there were strangled shrieks but Djokovic's backhand return was in, a forehand from Murray, a netted backhand from Djokovic.

Andy Murray, the champion, and Novak Djokovic, the runner-up, pose with their trophies

At the moment of victory, Murray dropped his racket, his mouth wide open in astonishment, before turning to the South West corner of Centre Court and pumping his fists in jubilation as the 15,000 privileged enough to witness this moment of history burst into an unprecedented roar of approval and spontaneous joy. Gallantly, Djokovic ran round the net to embrace the victor and then Britain's first men's singles champion for more than three quarters of a century walked back onto the court with his face in his hands before dropping to his knees where minutes earlier he had just played the match, and the game, of his life. And, unlike in New York, it had not taken him five sets. It just needed three, 6-4, 7-5, 6-4.

Seemingly unable to comprehend what he had achieved, nevertheless even in his greatest triumph, Murray did not forget where he was, asking the referee's permission to scale the stands to celebrate with everyone in his player's box. He almost forgot his mum Judy, however, who was busy being congratulated in the stands, but mother and son found each other to take the thunderous applause to a new crescendo and cause the shedding of yet more tears.

And then Andy Murray, Wimbledon champion, lifted the famous golden trophy – already engraved with his name alongside all those greats of the game – and Centre Court exploded with emotion once more.

Twelve months earlier, the tears had flowed in his post-match interview; this time, there were only smiles (even from Ivan Lendl) as the champion described winning Wimbledon as the "pinnacle of tennis".

It could not have been a nicer day had it tried.

WIMBLEDON IN NUMBERS

7 On the 7th of the 7th, Andy Murray ended a 77-year wait for a British Gentlemen's Singles champion at Wimbledon, also becoming the first British singles champion since Virginia Wade in the Silver Jubilee year of 1977.

"It's the pinnacle"

You said to us before that nothing would probably top the US Open. Are you changing your mind on that at all?

"I also said that winning Wimbledon I think is the pinnacle of tennis. I think the last game almost increased that feeling. It's the hardest few points I've had to play in my life. It was a different match to the US Open. Winning Wimbledon – I still can't believe it."

Any message for your hometown?

"I spoke to my grandparents on the phone. They were watching the match at the local sports club where I grew up playing. It was absolutely packed in there. Just thanks for always supporting me. I'm glad I managed to win this one for them."

Could you talk about what has been the key to your growth and success?

"I think I persevered. That's really been it – the story of my career probably. I had a lot of tough losses, but the one thing I would say is I think every year I always improved a little bit."

Nobody has ever heard noise like that at Wimbledon before. Did that surprise you?

"The atmosphere today was different to what I've experienced in the past. It was different to last year's final, for sure. And then the end of the match, that was incredibly loud, very noisy. I've been saying it all week, but it does make a difference. It really helps when the crowd's like that, the atmosphere is like that. Especially in a match as tough as that one where it's extremely hot, brutal, long rallies, tough games. They help you get through it."

Did you always feel this was going to happen, this day?

"No, I didn't always feel it was going to happen. It's incredibly difficult to win these events. I don't think that's that well understood sometimes. It takes so much hard work, mental toughness, to win these sorts of tournaments. I still can't believe it's happened. This one will take a little while to sink in, I'm sure."

The singles champions, Andy Murray and Marion Bartoli **(top)**, *with the Wimbledon trophies at the Champions' Dinner; Murray with coach Ivan Lendl* **(far left)**, *Bartoli* **(left)**, *and girlfriend Kim* **(below)**

The wait is over!

After 77 years of waiting for a men's singles champion at Wimbledon following Fred Perry's triumph in 1936, Britain needed no excuse to hold back the celebrations when Andy Murray finally got his hands on the most famous trophy in tennis.

At home, in pubs and clubs, and on the streets, Murray, the first British man to win the title wearing shorts, was the toast of the nation, as more than 17 millions viewers were glued to his historic triumph in what was the most-watched programme of 2013.

Prime Minister David Cameron suggested Murray should be knighted, the Royal Mail released a series of four special stamps commemorating his win, and the Royal Horticultural Society named a flower after him – Dahlia 'Andy Murray', a dark-stemmed dahlia with a golden flower. Murray's victory was even a talking point on EastEnders, which filmed a special scene for its episode two days after his triumph. To borrow a phrase from the BBC soap, everyone was talking about it.

(Above) Britain had to wait 77 years for a successor to Fred Perry, Wimbledon men's singles champion in 1934, 1935 and 1936

They said it!

"I can confirm that the Queen has sent a private message to Andy Murray following his Wimbledon victory."
Buckingham Palace spokeswoman

"It was a fantastic day for Andy Murray, for British tennis and for Britain. We were wondering, 'Do we dare to dream that this is possible?' and he proved absolutely that it was."
Prime Minister David Cameron

How times have changed

Much has changed since Britain last celebrated a men's singles champion at Wimbledon.

The Royal Mail issued a set of stamps to commemorate Murray's victory

	1936	2013
Prime Minister	Stanley Baldwin	David Cameron
Monarch	Edward VIII	Queen Elizabeth II
Pope	Pius XI	Francis I
Loaf of bread	4.5p	£1.32
Pint of beer	14p	£3.25
FA Cup winners	Arsenal	Wigan
Britain's Olympic standings	10th	3rd
Wimbledon ground pass	3 shillings	£8

"It's great for British tennis. Andy has worked his way up there. He deserves it. It's wonderful that he has won it and that he has played the way that he has. He has been playing beautiful tennis."
Fred Perry's son David

F J PERRY
WIMBLEDON CHAMPION
1934 1935 AND 1936

DAVID WYNNE
SCULPTOR 1984

Tweets

"A truly phenomenal victory by @andy_murray. Hard fought and well deserved. #Wimbledon"
Scottish First Minister Alex Salmond

"Oh my God. What a match, what a player. Inspiring a Nation. Andy Murray!! Ya Beauty."
Ewan McGregor

"What a privilege to experience that. Truly outstanding. Bravo Andy Murray."
Sir Chris Hoy

'What an incredible day!! So proud of my lil bro! What a champion!!'
Jamie Murray

Wimbledon 2013

Andy Murray
The Gentlemen's Singles

Marion Bartoli
The Ladies' Singles

Bob Bryan & Mike Bryan
The Gentlemen's Doubles

Hsieh Su-Wei & Peng Shuai
The Ladies' Doubles

Kristina Mladenovic & Daniel Nestor
The Mixed Doubles

The Champions

Gianluigi Quinzi
The Boys' Singles

Belinda Bencic
The Girls' Singles

Nick Kyrgios & Thanasi Kokkinakis
The Boys' Doubles

Barbora Krejcikova & Katerina Siniakova
The Girls' Doubles

**Mark Philippoussis &
Thomas Enqvist**
The Gentlemen's Invitation
Doubles

**Mark Woodforde &
Pat Cash**
The Gentlemen's Senior
Invitation Doubles

**Martina Hingis &
Lindsay Davenport**
The Ladies' Invitation
Doubles

Stephane Houdet & Shingo Kunieda
The Gentlemen's Wheelchair Doubles

Jiske Griffioen & Aniek Van Koot
The Ladies' Wheelchair Doubles

EVENT I – THE GENTLEMEN'S SINGLES CHAMPIONSHIP 2013

Holder: ROGER FEDERER

The Champion will become the holder, for the year only, of the CHALLENGE CUP presented by The All England Lawn Tennis and Croquet Club in 1887. The Champion will receive a silver three-quarter size replica of the Challenge Cup. A Silver Salver will be presented to the Runner up and a Bronze Medal to each defeated semi-finalist. The matches will be the best of three sets.

First Round

1. **Novak Djokovic [1]** *(1)* (SRB)
2. Florian Mayer *(34)* (GER)
3. (Q) Bobby Reynolds *(156)* (USA)
4. (WC) Steve Johnson *(98)* (USA)
5. Blaz Kavcic *(132)* (SLO)
6. (Q) Jan-Lennard Struff *(115)* (GER)
7. Ryan Harrison *(97)* (USA)
8. **Jeremy Chardy [28]** *(25)* (FRA)
9. **Gilles Simon [19]** *(17)* (FRA)
10. Feliciano Lopez *(32)* (ESP)
11. Ricardas Berankis *(69)* (LTU)
12. Paul-Henri Mathieu *(82)* (FRA)
13. (Q) Wayne Odesnik *(107)* (USA)
14. (Q) Jimmy Wang *(151)* (TPE)
15. Dmitry Tursunov *(65)* (RUS)
16. **Tommy Haas [13]** *(13)* (GER)
17. **Richard Gasquet [9]** *(9)* (FRA)
18. Marcel Granollers *(41)* (ESP)
19. Andreas Haider-Maurer *(108)* (AUT)
20. (Q) Go Soeda *(129)* (JPN)
21. James Blake *(87)* (USA)
22. Thiemo De Bakker *(93)* (NED)
23. Bernard Tomic *(59)* (AUS)
24. **Sam Querrey [21]** *(19)* (USA)
25. **Kevin Anderson [27]** *(23)* (RSA)
26. (LL) Olivier Rochus *(143)* (BEL)
27. Philipp Petzschner *(141)* (GER)
28. (Q) Michal Przysiezny *(127)* (POL)
29. Daniel Brands *(57)* (GER)
30. Daniel Gimeno-Traver *(56)* (ESP)
31. Martin Klizan *(36)* (SVK)
32. **Tomas Berdych [7]** *(6)* (CZE)
33. **David Ferrer [4]** *(4)* (ESP)
34. Martin Alund *(101)* (ARG)
35. Roberto Bautista Agut *(60)* (ESP)
36. (Q) Teymuraz Gabashvili *(137)* (RUS)
37. Horacio Zeballos *(52)* (ARG)
38. Santiago Giraldo *(91)* (COL)
39. Gastao Elias *(122)* (POR)
40. **Alexandr Dolgopolov [26]** *(24)* (UKR)
41. **Milos Raonic [17]** *(15)* (CAN)
42. Carlos Berlocq *(74)* (ARG)
43. (Q) Alex Kuznetsov *(173)* (USA)
44. Igor Sijsling *(64)* (NED)
45. (Q) James Duckworth *(174)* (AUS)
46. (Q) Denis Kudla *(105)* (USA)
47. Ivan Dodig *(49)* (CRO)
48. **Philipp Kohlschreiber [16]** *(18)* (GER)
49. **Kei Nishikori [12]** *(11)* (JPN)
50. (WC) Matthew Ebden *(110)* (AUS)
51. Leonardo Mayer *(84)* (ARG)
52. Aljaz Bedene *(90)* (SLO)
53. Michael Llodra *(53)* (FRA)
54. Jarkko Nieminen *(38)* (FIN)
55. Denis Istomin *(47)* (UZB)
56. **Andreas Seppi [23]** *(28)* (ITA)
57. **Grigor Dimitrov [29]** *(31)* (BUL)
58. Simone Bolelli *(89)* (ITA)
59. Grega Zemlja *(55)* (SLO)
60. Michael Russell *(95)* (USA)
61. Guido Pella *(76)* (ARG)
62. Jesse Levine *(112)* (CAN)
63. Albert Ramos *(62)* (ESP)
64. **Juan Martin Del Potro [8]** *(8)* (ARG)
65. **Rafael Nadal [5]** *(5)* (ESP)
66. Steve Darcis *(135)* (BEL)
67. Lukasz Kubot *(130)* (POL)
68. Igor Andreev *(108)* (RUS)
69. (Q) Stephane Robert *(165)* (FRA)
70. Alejandro Falla *(77)* (COL)
71. Adrian Ungur *(94)* (ROU)
72. **Benoit Paire [25]** *(27)* (FRA)
73. **John Isner [18]** *(21)* (USA)
74. Evgeny Donskoy *(66)* (RUS)
75. Pablo Andujar *(50)* (ESP)
76. Adrian Mannarino *(111)* (FRA)
77. (Q) Dustin Brown *(189)* (GER)
78. Guillermo Garcia-Lopez *(67)* (ESP)
79. Lleyton Hewitt *(70)* (AUS)
80. **Stanislas Wawrinka [11]** *(10)* (SUI)
81. **Nicolas Almagro [15]** *(16)* (ESP)
82. Jurgen Zopp *(88)* (EST)
83. Marinko Matosevic *(72)* (AUS)
84. Guillaume Rufin *(85)* (FRA)
85. Radek Stepanek *(45)* (CZE)
86. (Q) Matt Reid *(216)* (AUS)
87. (WC) Kyle Edmund *(385)* (GBR)
88. **Jerzy Janowicz [24]** *(22)* (POL)
89. **Fabio Fognini [30]** *(30)* (ITA)
90. Jurgen Melzer *(37)* (AUT)
91. (Q) Julian Reister *(121)* (GER)
92. Lukas Rosol *(35)* (CZE)
93. Rogerio Dutra Silva *(100)* (BRA)
94. Sergiy Stakhovsky *(116)* (UKR)
95. Victor Hanescu *(48)* (ROU)
96. **Roger Federer [3]** *(3)* (SUI)
97. **Jo-Wilfried Tsonga [6]** *(7)* (FRA)
98. David Goffin *(83)* (BEL)
99. Edouard Roger-Vasselin *(71)* (FRA)
100. Ernests Gulbis *(39)* (LAT)
101. Fernando Verdasco *(54)* (ESP)
102. Xavier Malisse *(61)* (BEL)
103. Tobias Kamke *(68)* (GER)
104. **Julien Benneteau [31]** *(33)* (FRA)
105. **Juan Monaco [22]** *(20)* (ARG)
106. (Q) Bastian Knittel *(210)* (GER)
107. Lukas Lacko *(79)* (SVK)
108. Rajeev Ram *(86)* (USA)
109. Kenny De Schepper *(80)* (FRA)
110. Paolo Lorenzi *(73)* (ITA)
111. Marcos Baghdatis *(40)* (CYP)
112. **Marin Cilic [10]** *(12)* (CRO)
113. **Janko Tipsarevic [14]** *(14)* (SRB)
114. Viktor Troicki *(44)* (SRB)
115. Andrey Kuznetsov *(78)* (RUS)
116. Albert Montanes *(51)* (ESP)
117. (Q) Marc Gicquel *(131)* (FRA)
118. Vasek Pospisil *(103)* (CAN)
119. Robin Haase *(58)* (NED)
120. **Mikhail Youzhny [20]** *(26)* (RUS)
121. **Tommy Robredo [32]** *(29)* (ESP)
122. Alex Bogomolov Jr. *(81)* (RUS)
123. (WC) Nicolas Mahut *(124)* (FRA)
124. Jan Hajek *(96)* (CZE)
125. (WC) James Ward *(219)* (GBR)
126. Yen-Hsun Lu *(75)* (TPE)
127. Benjamin Becker *(92)* (GER)
128. Andy Murray [2] *(2)* (GBR)

Second Round

- **Novak Djokovic [1]** 6/3 7/5 6/4
- Bobby Reynolds 1/6 7/6(4) 6/3 6/7(4) 6/4
- Jan-Lennard Struff 6/4 6/1 6/3
- **Jeremy Chardy [28]** 7/6(4) 4/6 7/5 6/2
- Feliciano Lopez 6/2 6/4 7/6(11)
- Paul-Henri Mathieu 7/6(4) 7/5 6/7(3) 6/4
- Jimmy Wang 7/6(5) 4/6 6/2 3/6 7/5
- **Tommy Haas [13]** 6/3 7/5 7/5
- **Richard Gasquet [9]** 6/7(2) 6/4 7/5 6/4
- Go Soeda 7/6(6) 7/5 6/1
- James Blake 6/1 6/3 6/2
- Bernard Tomic 7/6(6) 7/6(3) 3/6 2/6 6/3
- **Kevin Anderson [27]** 6/4 6/2 6/1
- Michal Przysiezny 6/3 7/6(6) 6/0
- Daniel Brands 7/6(5) 6/7(4) 6/7(5) 6/1 6/4
- **Tomas Berdych [7]** 6/3 6/4 6/4
- **David Ferrer [4]** 6/1 4/6 7/5 6/2
- Roberto Bautista Agut 6/3 6/4 7/6(3)
- Santiago Giraldo 3/6 7/6(4) 6/7(6) 6/1 6/3
- **Alexandr Dolgopolov [26]** 6/1 7/6(2) 6/2
- **Milos Raonic [17]** 6/4 6/3 6/3
- Igor Sijsling 6/3 6/4 6/4
- Denis Kudla 6/4 6/2 3/6 4/6 6/1
- Ivan Dodig 4/6 6/7(6) 7/6(3) 6/3 2/1 Ret'd
- **Kei Nishikori [12]** 6/2 6/4 6/3
- Leonardo Mayer 6/2 6/3 6/4
- Michael Llodra 7/6(3) 6/4 6/3
- **Andreas Seppi [23]** 7/6(6) 7/6(3) 5/7 3/6 6/3
- **Grigor Dimitrov [29]** 6/1 6/4 6/3
- Grega Zemlja 6/7(3) 6/4 6/4 6/1
- Jesse Levine 6/4 6/2 4/6 3/6 4/3 Ret'd
- **Juan Martin Del Potro [8]** 6/2 7/5 6/1
- Steve Darcis 7/6(4) 7/6(8) 6/4
- Lukasz Kubot 6/1 7/5 6/2
- Stephane Robert 6/3 7/6(5) 7/5
- **Benoit Paire [25]** 6/4 4/6 6/3 6/1
- **John Isner [18]** 6/1 7/6(5) 7/6(3)
- Adrian Mannarino 6/1 6/2 6/3
- Dustin Brown 6/3 6/3 6/3
- Lleyton Hewitt 6/4 7/5 6/3
- **Nicolas Almagro [15]** 6/4 7/6(2) 7/5
- Guillaume Rufin 6/1 4/6 6/4 6/3
- Radek Stepanek 6/2 6/2 6/4
- **Jerzy Janowicz [24]** 6/2 6/2 6/4
- Jurgen Melzer 6/7(5) 7/5 6/3 6/2
- Julian Reister 6/3 4/6 7/6(5) 6/7(4) 6/4
- Sergiy Stakhovsky 6/4 6/0 6/4
- **Roger Federer [3]** 6/3 6/2 6/0
- **Jo-Wilfried Tsonga [6]** 7/6(4) 6/4 6/3
- Ernests Gulbis 7/6(1) 6/4 7/5
- Fernando Verdasco 6/7(5) 6/1 6/4 6/3
- **Julien Benneteau [31]** 6/4 6/7(5) 6/4 6/2
- **Juan Monaco [22]** 6/4 6/2 6/3
- Rajeev Ram 7/5 6/4 6/7(2) 6/2
- Kenny De Schepper 7/6(6) 6/4 6/2
- **Marin Cilic [10]** 6/3 6/4 6/4
- Viktor Troicki 6/3 6/4 7/6(5)
- Andrey Kuznetsov 6/3 6/4 3/6 6/3
- Vasek Pospisil 6/3 6/2 7/6(3)
- **Mikhail Youzhny [20]** 6/4 7/5 7/5
- **Tommy Robredo [32]** 6/2 6/2 6/4
- Nicolas Mahut 6/2 6/4 6/3
- Yen-Hsun Lu 6/7(4) 6/4 7/6(11) 7/6(4)
- **Andy Murray [2]** 6/4 6/3 6/2

Third Round

- **Novak Djokovic [1]** 7/6(2) 6/3 6/1
- **Jeremy Chardy [28]** 6/2 5/7 7/6(6) 7/6(4)
- Feliciano Lopez 6/3 5/1 Ret'd
- **Tommy Haas [13]** 6/3 6/2 7/5
- **Richard Gasquet [9]** 6/0 6/3 6/7(5) 6/3
- Bernard Tomic 6/3 6/4 7/5
- **Kevin Anderson [27]** 6/4 7/6(2) 6/4
- **Tomas Berdych [7]** 7/6(6) 6/4 6/2
- **David Ferrer [4]** 6/3 3/6 7/6(4) 7/5
- **Alexandr Dolgopolov [26]** 6/4 7/5 6/3
- Igor Sijsling 7/5 6/4 7/6(4)
- Ivan Dodig 6/1 7/6(4) 7/5
- **Kei Nishikori [12]** 7/6(5) 6/4 6/2
- **Andreas Seppi [23]** 7/5 0/0 Ret'd
- Grega Zemlja 3/6 7/6(4) 3/6 6/4 11/9
- **Juan Martin Del Potro [8]** 6/2 7/6(7) 6/3
- Lukasz Kubot w/o
- **Benoit Paire [25]** 6/4 7/5 6/4
- Adrian Mannarino 1/1 Ret'd
- Dustin Brown 6/4 6/4 6/7(3) 6/2
- **Nicolas Almagro [15]** 7/5 6/7(6) 6/3 6/4
- **Jerzy Janowicz [24]** 6/2 5/3 Ret'd
- Jurgen Melzer 3/6 7/6(2) 7/6(5) 6/2
- Sergiy Stakhovsky 6/7(5) 7/6(5) 7/5 7/6(5)
- Ernests Gulbis 3/6 6/3 6/3 0/0 Ret'd
- Fernando Verdasco 7/6(1) 7/6(4) 6/4
- **Juan Monaco [22]** 5/7 6/2 6/4 6/2
- Kenny De Schepper w/o
- Viktor Troicki 6/4 6/3 6/4
- **Mikhail Youzhny [20]** 6/2 6/7(3) 7/6(7) 3/6 6/4
- **Tommy Robredo [32]** 7/6(3) 6/1 7/6(5)
- **Andy Murray [2]** 6/3 6/3 7/5

Fourth Round

- Novak Djokovic [1] 6/3 6/2 6/2
- Tommy Haas [13] 4/6 6/2 7/5 6/4
- Bernard Tomic 7/6(7) 5/7 7/5 7/6(5)
- Tomas Berdych [7] 3/6 6/3 6/4 7/5
- David Ferrer [4] 6/7(6) 7/6(2) 2/6 6/1 6/2
- Ivan Dodig 6/0 6/1 1/0 Ret'd
- Andreas Seppi [23] 3/6 6/2 6/7(4) 6/1 6/4
- Juan Martin Del Potro [8] 7/5 7/6(3) 6/0
- Lukasz Kubot 6/1 6/3 6/4
- Adrian Mannarino 6/4 6/2 7/5
- Jerzy Janowicz [24] 7/6(6) 6/3 6/4
- Jurgen Melzer 6/2 2/6 7/5 6/3
- Fernando Verdasco 6/2 6/4 6/4
- Kenny De Schepper 6/4 7/6(8) 6/4
- Mikhail Youzhny [20] 6/3 6/4 7/5
- Andy Murray [2] 6/2 6/4 7/5

Quarter-Finals

- Novak Djokovic [1] 6/1 6/4 7/6(4)
- Tomas Berdych [7] 7/6(4) 6/7(5) 6/4 6/4
- David Ferrer [4] 6/7(3) 7/6(6) 6/1 6/1
- Juan Martin Del Potro [8] 6/4 7/6(2) 6/3
- Lukasz Kubot 4/6 6/3 3/6 6/3 6/4
- Jerzy Janowicz [24] 3/6 7/6(1) 6/4 4/6 6/4
- Fernando Verdasco 6/4 6/4 6/4
- Andy Murray [2] 6/4 7/6(5) 6/1

Semi-Finals

- Novak Djokovic [1] 7/6(5) 6/4 6/3
- Juan Martin Del Potro [8] 6/2 6/4 7/6(5)
- Jerzy Janowicz [24] 7/5 6/4 6/4
- Andy Murray [2] 4/6 3/6 6/1 6/4 7/5

Final

- Novak Djokovic [1] 7/5 4/6 7/6(2) 6/7(6) 6/3
- Andy Murray [2] 6/7(2) 6/4 6/4 6/3

Champion: Andy Murray [2] 6/4 7/5 6/4

Heavy type denotes seeded players. The figure in brackets against names denotes the order in which they have been seeded. The figures in italics denotes ATP World Tour Ranking – 24/06/2013
(WC)=Wild card. (Q)=Qualifier. (LL)=Lucky loser.

EVENT II – THE GENTLEMEN'S DOUBLES CHAMPIONSHIP 2013
Holders: JONATHAN MARRAY & FREDERIK NIELSEN

The Champions will become the holders, for the year only, of the CHALLENGE CUPS presented by the OXFORD UNIVERSITY LAWN TENNIS CLUB in 1884 and the late SIR HERBERT WILBERFORCE in 1937. The Champions will receive a silver three-quarter size replica of the Challenge Cup. A Silver Salver will be presented to each of the Runners-up, and a Bronze Medal to each defeated semi-finalist. The matches will be the best of five sets.

First Round — *Second Round* — *Third Round* — *Quarter-Finals* — *Semi-Finals* — *Final*

1. **Bob Bryan** (USA) & **Mike Bryan** (USA) ....[1]
2. Marcelo Demoliner (BRA) & Andre Sa (BRA) ....
3. David Marrero (ESP) & Andreas Seppi (ITA) ....
(WC) 4. Jamie Baker (GBR) & Kyle Edmund (GBR)..............
(LL) 5. Denis Kudla (USA) & Tim Smyczek (USA) ....
6. Andre Begemann (GER) & Martin Emmrich (GER) ....
7. Roberto Bautista Agut (ESP) & Daniel Gimeno-Traver (ESP)..
8. **Treat Huey** (PHI) & **Dominic Inglot** (GBR)......[16]
9. **Santiago Gonzalez** (MEX) & **Scott Lipsky** (USA)..[10]
10. Paolo Lorenzi (ITA) & Benoit Paire (FRA)..............
11. Lukas Dlouhy (CZE) & Rajeev Ram (USA)..............
(Q) 12. Jesse Levine (CAN) & Vasek Pospisil (CAN)..............
(Q) 13. Purav Raja (IND) & Divij Sharan (IND) ....
14. Nicholas Monroe (USA) & Simon Stadler (GER) ......
15. Leonardo Mayer (ARG) & Albert Ramos (ESP) ......
16. **Mahesh Bhupathi** (IND) & **Julian Knowle** (AUT)..[8]
17. **Alexander Peya** (AUT) & **Bruno Soares** (BRA) ....[3]
18. Eric Butorac (USA) & Andy Ram (ISR) ....
19. Paul Hanley (AUS) & John-Patrick Smith (AUS) ......
20. Philipp Marx (GER) & Florin Mergea (ROU) ....
21. Fabio Fognini (ITA) & Potito Starace (ITA) ....
22. Daniel Brands (GER) & Lukas Rosol (CZE) ....
23. Jarkko Nieminen (FIN) & Dmitry Tursunov (RUS) ....
24. **Rohan Bopanna** (IND) & **Edouard Roger-Vasselin** (FRA)..[14]
25. **Colin Fleming** (GBR) & **Jonathan Marray** (GBR)....[9]
26. Martin Klizan (SVK) & Igor Zelenay (SVK)..............
27. Pablo Andujar (ESP) & Guillermo Garcia-Lopez (ESP)..
28. Frantisek Cermak (CZE) & Michal Mertinak (SVK)....
29. Robin Haase (NED) & Igor Sijsling (NED) ....
30. Eduardo Schwank (ARG) & Horacio Zeballos (ARG)..
31. Mikhail Elgin (RUS) & Denis Istomin (UZB)..............
32. **Robert Lindstedt** (SWE) & **Daniel Nestor** (CAN)[6]
33. **Aisam-Ul-Haq Qureshi** (PAK) & **Jean-Julien Rojer** (NED)..[5]
(LL) 34. Dustin Brown (GER) & Rameez Junaid (AUS) ....
35. Xavier Malisse (BEL) & Ken Skupski (GBR) ....
36. Evgeny Donskoy (RUS) & Andrey Kuznetsov (RUS)....
37. Grigor Dimitrov (BUL) & Frederik Nielsen (DEN)......
38. Bernard Tomic (AUS) & Viktor Troicki (SRB)..............
39. Lukas Lacko (SVK) & Filip Polasek (SVK)..............
40. **Julien Benneteau** (FRA) & **Nenad Zimonjic** (SRB)..[11]
41. **Lukasz Kubot** (POL) & **Marcin Matkowski** (POL)..[15]
42. Johan Brunstrom (SWE) & Raven Klaasen (RSA)....
(WC) 43. David Rice (GBR) & Sean Thornley (GBR)..............
44. Marinko Matosevic (AUS) & Frank Moser (GER) ......
45. Jamie Delgado (GBR) & Matthew Ebden (AUS) ......
(WC) 46. Lleyton Hewitt (AUS) & Mark Knowles (BAH) ....
47. Daniele Bracciali (ITA) & Jonathan Erlich (ISR) ......
48. **Leander Paes** (IND) & **Radek Stepanek** (CZE)..[4]
49. **Max Mirnyi** (BLR) & **Horia Tecau** (ROU)......[7]
(Q) 50. Dominik Meffert (GER) & Philipp Oswald (AUT)......
(Q) 51. Samuel Groth (AUS) & Chris Guccione (AUS)............
(LL) 52. Steve Johnson (USA) & Andreas Siljestrom (SWE)..
53. Ricardas Berankis (LTU) & Yen-Hsun Lu (TPE)........
54. Tomasz Bednarek (POL) & Mateusz Kowalczyk (POL)..
55. Santiago Giraldo (COL) & Michael Russell (USA) ....
56. **Ivan Dodig** (CRO) & **Marcelo Melo** (BRA)......[12]
57. **Michael Llodra** (FRA) & **Nicolas Mahut** (FRA)..[13]
58. Jan Hajek (CZE) & Jaroslav Levinsky (CZE)..............
59. James Blake (USA) & Jurgen Melzer (AUT) ....
60. Jamie Murray (GBR) & John Peers (AUS)..............
61. Aljaz Bedene (SLO) & Grega Zemlja (SLO)................
62. Sanchai Ratiwatana (THA) & Sonchat Ratiwatana (THA)..
63. Juan Sebastian Cabal (COL) & Robert Farah (COL)..
64. **Marcel Granollers** (ESP) & **Marc Lopez** (ESP)......[2]

Second Round:
Bob Bryan & Mike Bryan [1] — 6/4 6/4 6/1
David Marrero & Andreas Seppi — 6/4 7/5 6/2
Andre Begemann & Martin Emmrich — 6/2 6/7(4) 6/4 6/1
Treat Huey & Dominic Inglot [16] — 6/3 6/4 7/5
Santiago Gonzalez & Scott Lipsky [10] — 6/4 7/6(3) 6/4
Jesse Levine & Vasek Pospisil — 6/2 6/4 6/1
Nicholas Monroe & Simon Stadler — 6/7(4) 2/6 6/3 6/4 6/4
Mahesh Bhupathi & Julian Knowle [8] — 6/2 6/7(5) 6/4 6/2
Alexander Peya & Bruno Soares [3] — 6/4 3/6 6/3 6/4
Paul Hanley & John-Patrick Smith — 6/3 1/6 7/6(5) 6/4
Daniel Brands & Lukas Rosol — 6/4 6/4 6/4
Rohan Bopanna & Edouard Roger-Vasselin [14] — 7/6(5) 6/2 7/6(6)
Colin Fleming & Jonathan Marray [9] — 7/6(4) 4/6 6/3 6/4
Frantisek Cermak & Michal Mertinak — 6/7(7) 6/7(5) 6/4 7/5 6/2
Eduardo Schwank & Horacio Zeballos — 6/4 6/7(7) 6/3 6/4
Robert Lindstedt & Daniel Nestor [6] — 7/6(6) 6/3 6/7(9) 7/6(2)
Aisam Qureshi & Jean-Julien Rojer [5] — 7/6(5) 6/4 6/4
Xavier Malisse & Ken Skupski — 7/6(5) 6/7(4) 6/0 6/1
Grigor Dimitrov & Frederik Nielsen — 6/3 1/2 Ret'd
Julien Benneteau & Nenad Zimonjic [11] — 3/6 6/3 6/7(4) 6/2 6/1
Lukasz Kubot & Marcin Matkowski [15] — 6/3 6/4 7/5
Marinko Matosevic & Frank Moser — 6/4 6/3 6/7(7) 4/6 6/4
Jamie Delgado & Matthew Ebden — 6/3 7/5 7/6(4)
Leander Paes & Radek Stepanek [4] — 7/6(6) 6/4 6/7(1) 6/4
Max Mirnyi & Horia Tecau [7] — 4/6 7/5 6/3 6/4
Samuel Groth & Chris Guccione — 7/6(5) 7/6(6) 6/3
Tomasz Bednarek & Mateusz Kowalczyk — 6/2 6/4 6/1
Ivan Dodig & Marcelo Melo [12] — 6/3 7/6(3) 6/2
Michael Llodra & Nicolas Mahut [13] — 5/4 Ret'd
James Blake & Jurgen Melzer — 3/6 6/4 3/6 14/12
Sanchai Ratiwatana & Sonchat Ratiwatana — 6/3 6/4 5/7 7/6(3)
Juan-Sebastian Cabal & Robert Farah — 6/7(1) 7/5 7/5 7/6(5)

Third Round:
Bob Bryan & Mike Bryan [1] — 6/3 7/5 6/4
Treat Huey & Dominic Inglot [16] — 6/3 6/7(2) 7/5 7/6(3)
Jesse Levine & Vasek Pospisil — 4/6 7/6(3) 6/4 3/6 6/3
Mahesh Bhupathi & Julian Knowle [8] — 3/6 6/4 6/4 6/2
Alexander Peya & Bruno Soares [3] — 4/6 6/1 6/7(6) 7/5 10/8
Rohan Bopanna & Edouard Roger-Vasselin [14] — 6/3 5/7 7/6(4) 6/7(8) 6/4
Colin Fleming & Jonathan Marray [9] — 6/3 6/4 7/6(7)
Robert Lindstedt & Daniel Nestor [6] — 6/1 7/5 6/3
Aisam Qureshi & Jean-Julien Rojer [5] — 6/3 6/7(1) 6/3 6/7(5) 8/6
Julien Benneteau & Nenad Zimonjic [11] — 6/7(3) 6/3 5/7 6/2 8/6
Lukasz Kubot & Marcin Matkowski [15] — 2/6 4/6 6/2 6/2 6/1
Leander Paes & Radek Stepanek [4] — 6/4 6/4 6/3
Max Mirnyi & Horia Tecau [7] — 6/4 7/6(6) 7/6(2) 7/5
Ivan Dodig & Marcelo Melo [12] — 7/6(2) 7/5 6/4
James Blake & Jurgen Melzer — 6/4 6/0 6/1
Juan-Sebastian Cabal & Robert Farah — 3/6 7/6(5) 3/6 6/3 6/4

Quarter-Finals:
Bob Bryan & Mike Bryan [1] — 7/5 6/3 7/6(3)
Mahesh Bhupathi & Julian Knowle [8] — 6/2 6/4 3/6 6/4
Rohan Bopanna & Edouard Roger-Vasselin [14] — 6/4 4/6 7/6(5) 6/2
Robert Lindstedt & Daniel Nestor [6] — 7/6(5) 7/5 6/3
Julien Benneteau & Nenad Zimonjic [11] — 3/6 4/6 7/6(1) 7/6(4) 6/3
Leander Paes & Radek Stepanek [4] — 6/4 6/2 6/4
Ivan Dodig & Marcelo Melo [12] — 6/7(6) 2/6 6/4 6/2 6/4
James Blake & Jurgen Melzer — 6/2 6/4 6/3

Semi-Finals:
Bob Bryan & Mike Bryan [1] — 7/6(5) 7/6(3) 7/6(4)
Rohan Bopanna & Edouard Roger-Vasselin [14] — 7/5 7/6(3) 6/7(4) 6/7(3) 6/2
Leander Paes & Radek Stepanek [4] — 4/6 6/4 6/3 6/4
Ivan Dodig & Marcelo Melo [12] — 7/5 6/0 6/7(10) 6/4

Final:
Bob Bryan & Mike Bryan [1] — 6/7(4) 6/4 6/3 5/7 6/3
Ivan Dodig & Marcelo Melo [12] — 3/6 6/4 6/1 3/6 6/3

Bob Bryan & Mike Bryan [1] — 3/6 6/3 6/4 6/4

Heavy type denotes seeded players. The figure in brackets against names denotes the order in which they have been seeded.
(WC)=Wild card. (Q)=Qualifier. (LL)=Lucky loser.

EVENT III – THE LADIES' SINGLES CHAMPIONSHIP 2013
Holder: SERENA WILLIAMS

The Champion will become the holder, for the year only, of the CHALLENGE TROPHY presented by The All England Lawn Tennis and Croquet Club in 1886. The Champion will receive a silver three-quarter size replica of the Challenge Trophy. A Silver Salver will be presented to the Runner up and a Bronze Medal to each defeated semi-finalist. The matches will be the best of three sets.

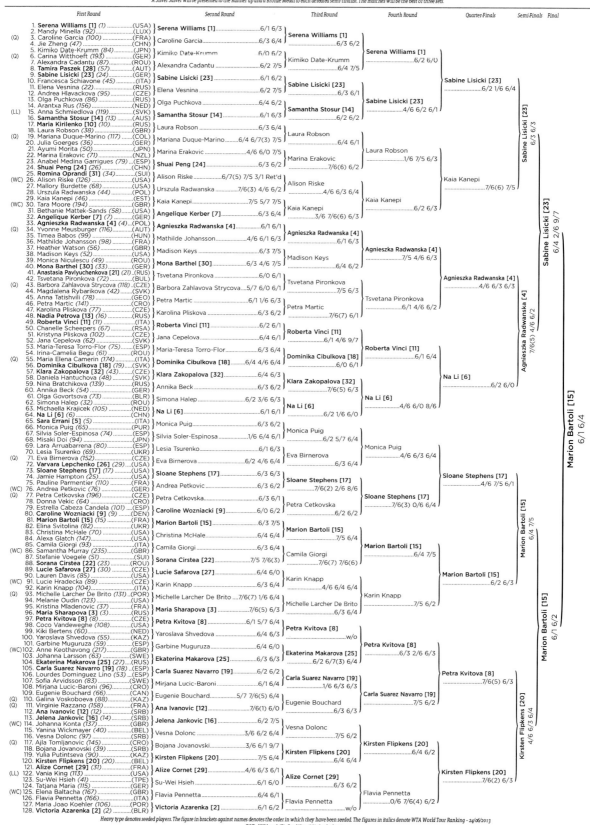

Heavy type denotes seeded players. The figure in brackets against names denotes the order in which they have been seeded. The figures in italics denote WTA World Tour Ranking – 24/06/2013
(WC)=Wild card. (Q)=Qualifier. (LL)=Lucky loser.

EVENT IV – THE LADIES' DOUBLES CHAMPIONSHIP 2013
Holders: SERENA WILLIAMS & VENUS WILLIAMS

The Champions will become the holders, for the year only, of the CHALLENGE CUPS presented by H.R.H. PRINCESS MARINA, DUCHESS OF KENT, the late President of The All England Lawn Tennis and Croquet Club in 1949 and The All England Lawn Tennis and Croquet Club in 2001. Champions will receive a silver three-quarter size replica of the Challenge Cup. A Silver Salver will be presented to each of the Runners-up and a Bronze Medal to each defeated semi-finalist. The matches will be the best of three sets.

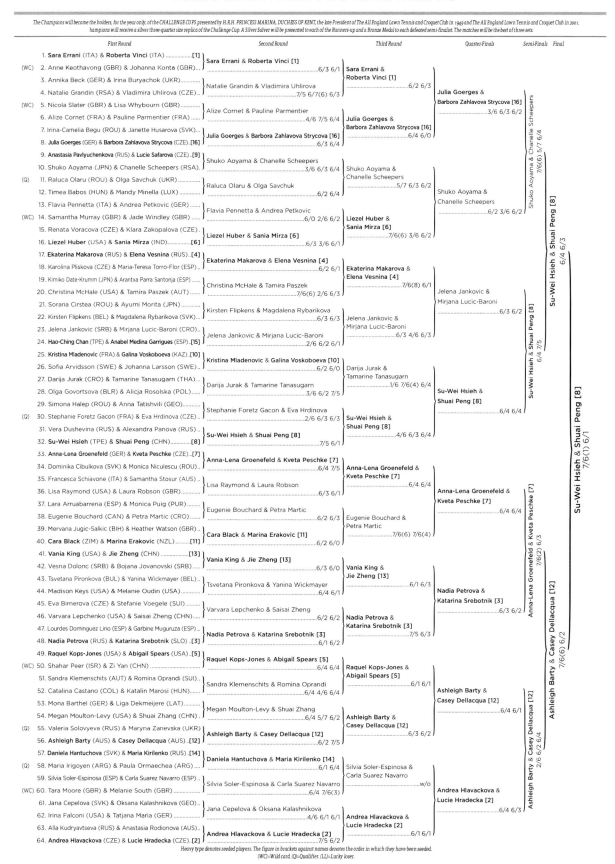

Heavy type denotes seeded players. The figure in brackets against names denotes the order in which they have been seeded.
(WC)=Wild card. (Q)=Qualifier. (LL)=Lucky loser.

EVENT V – THE MIXED DOUBLES CHAMPIONSHIP 2013
Holders: MIKE BRYAN & LISA RAYMOND

The Champions will become the holders, for the year only, of the CHALLENGE CUPS presented by members of the family of the late Mr. S. H. SMITH in 1949 and The All England Lawn Tennis and Croquet Club in 2001. The Champions will receive a silver three-quarter size replica of the Challenge Cup. A Silver Salver will be presented to each of the Runners-up and a Bronze Medal to each defeated semi-finalist. The matches will be the best of three sets.

First Round	Second Round	Third Round	Quarter-Finals	Semi-Finals	Final

1. **Bruno Soares** (BRA) & **Lisa Raymond** (USA)....[1]
2. Bye
3. Colin Fleming (GBR) & Laura Robson (GBR)
4. Filip Polasek (SVK) & Janette Husarova (SVK)

Bruno Soares & Lisa Raymond [1]

Filip Polasek & Janette Husarova
..................6/7(2) 6/2 6/4

Bruno Soares & Lisa Raymond [1]
..................6/2 6/3

(WC) 5. Kyle Edmund (GBR) & Eugenie Bouchard (CAN)
6. Frederik Nielsen (DEN) & Sofia Arvidsson (SWE)
7. Bye
8. **Ivan Dodig** (CRO) & **Marina Erakovic** (NZL)...[16]

Frederik Nielsen & Sofia Arvidsson
..................7/5 6/4

Ivan Dodig & Marina Erakovic [16]

Frederik Nielsen & Sofia Arvidsson
..................3/6 6/3 6/4

Bruno Soares & Lisa Raymond [1]
..................6/3 6/4

9. **Treat Huey** (PHI) & **Raquel Kops-Jones** (USA)...[9]
10. Bye
11. Julian Knowle (AUT) & Shuai Zhang (CHN)
12. John Peers (AUS) & Ashleigh Barty (AUS)

Treat Huey & Raquel Kops-Jones [9]

John Peers & Ashleigh Barty
..................6/7(7) 6/3 6/3

John Peers & Ashleigh Barty
..................4/6 6/3 6/4

John Peers & Ashleigh Barty
..................6/4 1/6 6/2

13. Rajeev Ram (USA) & Francesca Schiavone (ITA)
14. Raven Klaasen (RSA) & Anastasia Rodionova (AUS)
15. Bye
16. **Marcelo Melo** (BRA) & **Liezel Huber** (USA)...[6]

Rajeev Ram & Francesca Schiavone
..................7/6(6) 4/6 6/4

Marcelo Melo & Liezel Huber [6]

Marcelo Melo & Liezel Huber [6]
..................4/0 Ret'd

Bruno Soares & Lisa Raymond [1]
..................7/6(6) 7/6(4)

17. **Max Mirnyi** (BLR) & **Andrea Hlavackova** (CZE)...[4]
18. Bye
19. Jean-Julien Rojer (NED) & Vera Dushevina (RUS)
20. Jamie Murray (GBR) & Su-Wei Hsieh (TPE)

Max Mirnyi & Andrea Hlavackova [4]

Jean-Julien Rojer & Vera Dushevina
..................6/7(2) 6/3 6/4

Jean-Julien Rojer & Vera Dushevina
..................7/6(3) 6/3

Jean-Julien Rojer & Vera Dushevina
..................6/7(4) 7/6(3) 7/5

21. Robin Haase (NED) & Alicja Rosolska (POL)
22. Jonathan Marray (GBR) & Heather Watson (GBR)
23. Bye
24. David Marrero (ESP) & Kimiko Date-Krumm (JPN)...[14]

Jonathan Marray & Heather Watson
..................6/3 7/5

David Marrero & Kimiko Date-Krumm [14]

David Marrero & Kimiko Date-Krumm [14]
..................2/6 6/3 6/3

Jean-Julien Rojer & Vera Dushevina
..................6/3 3/6 6/3

25. **Frantisek Cermak** (CZE) & **Lucie Hradecka** (CZE)...[12]
26. Bye
(A) 27. James Cerretani (USA) & Mona Barthel (GER)
28. Johan Brunstrom (SWE) & Katalin Marosi (HUN)

Frantisek Cermak & Lucie Hradecka [12]

Johan Brunstrom & Katalin Marosi
..................3/6 6/3 6/3

Johan Brunstrom & Katalin Marosi
..................7/6(3) 6/3

Rohan Bopanna & Jie Zheng [7]
..................7/6(4) 3/6 6/1

29. Paul Hanley (AUS) & Hao-Ching Chan (TPE)
30. Robert Farah (COL) & Darija Jurak (CRO)
31. Bye
32. **Rohan Bopanna** (IND) & **Jie Zheng** (CHN)..........[7]

Robert Farah & Darija Jurak
..................6/2 6/4

Rohan Bopanna & Jie Zheng [7]

Rohan Bopanna & Jie Zheng [7]
..................7/6(6) 7/5

33. **Alexander Peya** (AUT) & **Anna-Lena Groenefeld** (GER)...[5]
34. Bye
35. Nicholas Monroe (USA) & Marion Bartoli (FRA)
36. Santiago Gonzalez (MEX) & Natalie Grandin (RSA)

Alexander Peya & Anna-Lena Groenefeld [5]

Santiago Gonzalez & Natalie Grandin
..................6/4 4/6 6/1

Alexander Peya & Anna-Lena Groenefeld [5]
..................6/2 6/4

Marcin Matkowski & Kveta Peschke [11]
..................6/7(3) 6/4 6/2

37. Andy Ram (ISR) & Abigail Spears (USA)
38. Daniele Bracciali (ITA) & Galina Voskoboeva (KAZ)
39. Bye
40. **Marcin Matkowski** (POL) & **Kveta Peschke** (CZE)...[11]

Andy Ram & Abigail Spears
..................6/4 6/7(6) 6/2

Marcin Matkowski & Kveta Peschke [11]

Marcin Matkowski & Kveta Peschke [11]
..................7/5 7/5

Nenad Zimonjic & Katarina Srebotnik [3]
..................7/6(10) 6/7(6) 6/4

41. **Scott Lipsky** (USA) & **Casey Dellacqua** (AUS)...[13]
42. Bye
43. Fabio Fognini (ITA) & Flavia Pennetta (ITA)
(WC) 44. Jamie Delgado (GBR) & Tara Moore (GBR)

Scott Lipsky & Casey Dellacqua [13]

Fabio Fognini & Flavia Pennetta
..................7/6(2) 6/3

Scott Lipsky & Casey Dellacqua [13]
..................w/o

Nenad Zimonjic & Katarina Srebotnik [3]
..................6/2 6/7(3) 6/2

(WC) 45. James Blake (USA) & Donna Vekic (CRO)
(A) 46. Jaroslav Levinsky (CZE) & Liga Dekmeijere (LAT)
47. Bye
48. **Nenad Zimonjic** (SRB) & **Katarina Srebotnik** (SLO)...[3]

James Blake & Donna Vekic
..................6/4 6/1

Nenad Zimonjic & Katarina Srebotnik [3]

Nenad Zimonjic & Katarina Srebotnik [3]
..................7/5 6/1

49. **Daniel Nestor** (CAN) & **Kristina Mladenovic** (FRA)...[8]
50. Bye
(WC) 51. Dominic Inglot (GBR) & Johanna Konta (GBR)
52. Nicolas Almagro (ESP) & Maria-Teresa Torro-Flor (ESP)

Daniel Nestor & Kristina Mladenovic [8]

Dominic Inglot & Johanna Konta
..................4/6 6/3 19/17

Daniel Nestor & Kristina Mladenovic [8]
..................3/6 6/3 6/2

Daniel Nestor & Kristina Mladenovic [8]
..................3/6 6/3 6/2

53. Mahesh Bhupathi (IND) & Daniela Hantuchova (SVK)
(WC) 54. Mark Knowles (BAH) & Sabine Lisicki (GER)
55. Bye
56. **Aisam Qureshi** (PAK) & **Cara Black** (ZIM)...[10]

Mark Knowles & Sabine Lisicki
..................6/7(2) 6/4 6/4

Aisam Qureshi & Cara Black [10]

Aisam Qureshi & Cara Black [10]
..................w/o

Daniel Nestor & Kristina Mladenovic [8]
..................7/6(5) 7/6(5)

57. **Leander Paes** (IND) & **Saisai Zheng** (CHN)...[15]
58. Bye
59. Michal Mertinak (SVK) & Vladimira Uhlirova (CZE)
60. Eric Butorac (USA) & Alize Cornet (FRA)

Leander Paes & Saisai Zheng [15]

Eric Butorac & Alize Cornet
..................6/4 3/6 6/3

Eric Butorac & Alize Cornet
..................6/3 6/3

Horia Tecau & Sania Mirza [2]
..................6/1 7/5

61. Martin Emmrich (GER) & Julia Goerges (GER)
62. Juan-Sebastian Cabal (COL) & Bojana Jovanovski (SRB)
63. Bye
64. **Horia Tecau** (ROU) & **Sania Mirza** (IND)...........[2]

Martin Emmrich & Julia Goerges
..................7/5 6/2

Horia Tecau & Sania Mirza [2]

Horia Tecau & Sania Mirza [2]
..................6/3 6/4

Semi-Finals / Final:

Bruno Soares & Lisa Raymond [1]
..................6/4 6/4

Daniel Nestor & Kristina Mladenovic [8]
..................6/2 6/7(4) 11/9

Daniel Nestor & Kristina Mladenovic [8]
..................5/7 6/2 8/6

Heavy type denotes seeded players. The figure in brackets against names denotes the order in which they have been seeded.
(A)=Alternate. (WC)=Wild card.

EVENT VI – THE BOYS' SINGLES CHAMPIONSHIP 2013
Holder: FILIP PELIWO

The Champion will become the holder, for the year only, of a Cup presented by The All England Lawn Tennis and Croquet Club. The Champion will receive a three-quarter size Cup and the Runner-up will receive a Silver Salver. The matches will be best of three sets.

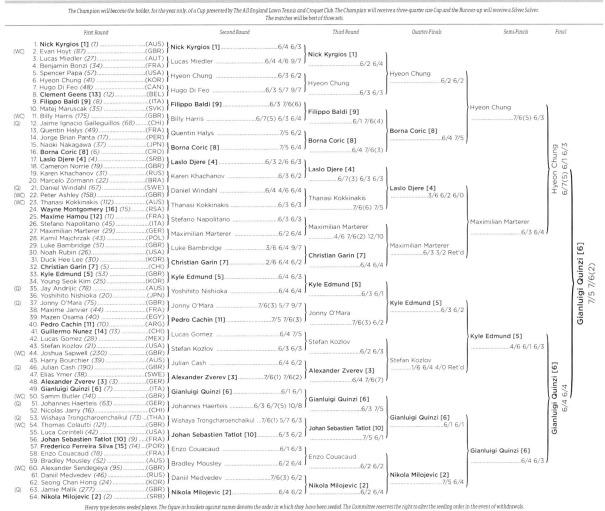

First Round	Second Round	Third Round	Quarter-Finals	Semi-Finals	Final

1. Nick Kyrgios [1] (1) ....(AUS)
(WC) 2. Evan Hoyt (87) ....(GBR)
3. Lucas Miedler (27) ....(AUT)
4. Benjamin Bonzi (34) ....(FRA)
5. Spencer Papa (57) ....(USA)
6. Hyeon Chung (41) ....(KOR)
7. Hugo Di Feo (48) ....(CAN)
8. Clement Geens [13] (12) ....(BEL)
9. Filippo Baldi [9] (8) ....(ITA)
10. Matej Maruscak (35) ....(SVK)
(WC) 11. Billy Harris (175) ....(GBR)
(Q) 12. Jaime Ignacio Galleguillos (68) ....(CHI)
13. Quentin Halys (49) ....(FRA)
14. Jorge Brian Panta (17) ....(PER)
15. Naoki Nakagawa (37) ....(JPN)
16. Borna Coric [8] (6) ....(CRO)
17. Laslo Djere [4] (4) ....(SRB)
18. Cameron Norrie (19) ....(GBR)
19. Karen Khachanov (31) ....(RUS)
20. Marcelo Zormann (22) ....(BRA)
(Q) 21. Daniel Windahl (67) ....(SWE)
(WC) 22. Peter Ashley (158) ....(GBR)
(WC) 23. Thanasi Kokkinakis (112) ....(AUS)
24. Wayne Montgomery [16] (15) ....(RSA)
25. Maxime Hamou [12] (11) ....(FRA)
26. Stefano Napolitano (45) ....(ITA)
27. Maximilian Marterer (29) ....(GER)
28. Kamil Majchrzak (43) ....(POL)
29. Luke Bambridge (51) ....(GBR)
30. Noah Rubin (26) ....(USA)
31. Duck Hee Lee (30) ....(KOR)
32. Christian Garin [7] (5) ....(CHI)
33. Kyle Edmund [5] (53) ....(GBR)
34. Young Seok Kim (25) ....(KOR)
(Q) 35. Jay Andrijic (78) ....(AUS)
36. Yoshihito Nishioka (20) ....(JPN)
(Q) 37. Jonny O'Mara (75) ....(GBR)
38. Maxime Janvier (44) ....(FRA)
39. Mazen Osama (40) ....(EGY)
40. Pedro Cachin [11] (10) ....(ARG)
41. Guillermo Nunez [14] (13) ....(CHI)
42. Lucas Gomez (28) ....(MEX)
43. Stefan Kozlov (21) ....(USA)
(WC) 44. Joshua Sapwell (230) ....(GBR)
45. Harry Bourchier (39) ....(AUS)
(Q) 46. Julian Cash (190) ....(GBR)
47. Elias Ymer (38) ....(SWE)
48. Alexander Zverev [3] (3) ....(GER)
49. Gianluigi Quinzi [6] (7) ....(ITA)
(WC) 50. Samm Butler (141) ....(GBR)
(Q) 51. Johannes Haerteis (63) ....(GER)
52. Nicolas Jarry (16) ....(CHI)
(Q) 53. Wishaya Trongcharoenchaikul (73) ....(THA)
(WC) 54. Thomas Colautti (121) ....(GBR)
55. Luca Corinteli (42) ....(USA)
56. Johan Sebastien Tatlot [10] (9) ......(FRA)
57. Frederico Ferreira Silva [15] (14) ....(POR)
58. Enzo Couacaud (18) ....(FRA)
59. Bradley Mousley (52) ....(AUS)
(WC) 60. Alexander Sendegeya (95) ....(GBR)
61. Daniil Medvedev (46) ....(RUS)
62. Seong Chan Hong (24) ....(KOR)
(Q) 63. Jamie Malik (277) ....(GBR)
64. Nikola Milojevic [2] (2) ....(SRB)

Second Round:
Nick Kyrgios [1] 6/4 6/3
Lucas Miedler 6/4 4/6 9/7
Hyeon Chung 6/3 6/2
Hugo Di Feo 6/3 5/7 9/7
Filippo Baldi [9] ...... 6/3 7/6(6)
Billy Harris ...... 6/7(5) 6/3 6/4
Quentin Halys 7/5 6/2
Borna Coric [8] 7/5 6/4
Laslo Djere [4] 6/3 2/6 6/3
Karen Khachanov 6/3 6/2
Daniel Windahl 6/4 4/6 6/4
Thanasi Kokkinakis 6/3 6/3
Stefano Napolitano 6/3 6/3
Maximilian Marterer 6/2 6/4
Luke Bambridge 3/6 6/4 9/7
Christian Garin [7] 2/6 6/4 6/2
Kyle Edmund [5] 6/4 6/3
Yoshihito Nishioka 6/4 6/4
Jonny O'Mara ...... 7/6(3) 5/7 9/7
Pedro Cachin [11] ...... 7/5 7/6(3)
Lucas Gomez 6/4 7/5
Stefan Kozlov 6/3 6/3
Julian Cash 6/4 6/2
Alexander Zverev [3] ...... 7/6(1) 7/6(2)
Gianluigi Quinzi [6] 6/1 6/1
Johannes Haerteis ...... 6/3 6/7(5) 10/8
Wishaya Trongcharoenchaikul ...7/6(1) 5/7 6/3
Johan Sebastien Tatlot [10] 6/3 6/2
Enzo Couacaud 6/1 6/3
Bradley Mousley 6/2 6/4
Daniil Medvedev ...... 7/6(3) 6/2
Nikola Milojevic [2] 6/4 6/2

Third Round:
Nick Kyrgios [1] 6/2 6/4
Hyeon Chung 6/3 6/3
Filippo Baldi [9] ...... 6/1 7/6(4)
Borna Coric [8] ...... 6/4 7/6(3)
Laslo Djere [4] ...... 6/7(3) 6/3 6/3
Thanasi Kokkinakis ...... 7/6(6) 7/5
Maximilian Marterer ...... 4/7 7/6(2) 12/10
Christian Garin [7] 6/4 6/4
Kyle Edmund [5] 6/3 6/1
Jonny O'Mara ...... 7/6(3) 6/2
Stefan Kozlov 6/2 6/3
Alexander Zverev [3] ...... 6/4 7/6(7)
Gianluigi Quinzi [6] 6/3 7/5
Johan Sebastien Tatlot [10] 7/5 6/1
Enzo Couacaud 6/2 6/2
Nikola Milojevic [2] 6/2 6/4

Quarter-Finals:
Hyeon Chung 6/2 6/2
Borna Coric [8] 6/4 7/5
Laslo Djere [4] 3/6 6/2 6/0
Maximilian Marterer ...... 6/3 3/2 Ret'd
Kyle Edmund [5] 6/3 6/2
Stefan Kozlov ...... 1/6 6/4 4/0 Ret'd
Gianluigi Quinzi [6] 6/1 6/1
Nikola Milojevic [2] 7/5 6/4

Semi-Finals:
Hyeon Chung ...... 7/6(5) 6/3
Maximilian Marterer 6/3 6/4
Kyle Edmund [5] 4/6 6/1 6/3
Gianluigi Quinzi [6] 6/4 6/3

Semi-Finals (next column):
Hyeon Chung ...... 6/7(5) 6/1 6/3
Gianluigi Quinzi [6] ...... 7/5 7/6(2)

Final:
Gianluigi Quinzi [6] ...... 7/5 7/6(2)

Heavy type denotes seeded players. The figure in brackets against names denotes the order in which they have been seeded. The Committee reserves the right to alter the seeding order in the event of withdrawals.
(WC) = Wild card. (Q) = Qualifier. (LL) = Lucky Loser.

EVENT VII – THE BOYS' DOUBLES CHAMPIONSHIP 2013
Holders: ANDREW HARRIS & NICK KYRGIOS

The Champions will become the holders, for the year only, of a Cup presented by The All England Lawn Tennis and Croquet Club. The Champions will receive a three-quarter size Cup and the Runners-up will receive a Silver Salvers. The matches will be best of three sets.

First Round	Second Round	Quarter-Finals	Semi-Finals	Final

1. Kyle Edmund (GBR) & Frederico Ferreira Silva (POR)...[1]
2. Daniel Windahl (SWE) & Elias Ymer (SWE)..............
(WC) 3. Samm Butler (GBR) & Billy Harris (GBR)..............
4. Maximilian Marterer (GER) & Lucas Miedler (AUT)...
5. Luca Corinteli (USA) & Lucas Gomez (MEX)..............
6. Hyeon Chung (KOR) & Duck Hee Lee (KOR)..............
(WC) 7. Peter Ashley (GBR) & Alexander Sendegeya (GBR)....
8. Clement Geens (BEL) & Noah Rubin (USA)..........[6]
9. Christian Garin (CHI) & Nicolas Jarry (CHI)..........[3]
10. Benjamin Bonzi (FRA) & Quentin Halys (FRA)..........
11. Evan Hoyt (GBR) & Wayne Montgomery (RSA)..........
12. Jay Andrijic (AUS) & Bradley Mousley (AUS)..........
13. Stefan Kozlov (USA) & Spencer Papa (USA)..........
(WC) 14. Julian Cash (GBR) & Joshua Sapwell (GBR)..........
15. Enzo Couacaud (FRA) & Stefano Napolitano (ITA)....
16. Naoki Nakagawa (JPN) & Gianluigi Quinzi (ITA)..[7]
17. Yoshihito Nishioka (JPN) & Jorge Brian Panta (PER)...[5]
18. Seong Chan Hong (KOR) & Young Seok Kim (KOR)...
19. Maxime Janvier (FRA) & Kamil Majchrzak (POL)......
20. Luke Bambridge (GBR) & Cameron Norrie (GBR)......
21. Thanasi Kokkinakis (AUS) & Nick Kyrgios (AUS)......
22. Rafael Matos (BRA) & Marcelo Zormann (BRA)........
23. Hugo Di Feo (CAN) & Mazen Osama (EGY)............
(WC) 24. Pedro Cachin (ARG) & Guillermo Nunez (CHI)....[4]
(A) 25. Johannes Haerteis (GER) & Hannes Wagner (GER)..
26. Cem Ilkel (TUR) & Matej Maruscak (SVK)..............
(WC) 27. Jamie Malik (GBR) & Robbie Ridout (GBR)............
28. Laslo Djere (SRB) & Martin Redlicki (USA)..........
29. Borna Coric (CRO) & Jonny O'Mara (GBR)............
30. Filippo Baldi (ITA) & Matteo Donati (ITA)............
31. Karen Khachanov (RUS) & Daniil Medvedev (RUS)...
32. Maxime Hamou (FRA) & Johan Sebastien Tatlot (FRA)...[2]

Second Round:
Kyle Edmund & Frederico Ferreira Silva [1] ...7/5 4/6 6/3
Maximilian Marterer & Lucas Miedler 6/4 6/4
Luca Corinteli & Lucas Gomez 6/3 4/6 6/2
Clement Geens & Noah Rubin [6] 6/3 6/3
Benjamin Bonzi & Quentin Halys ......w/o
Jay Andrijic & Bradley Mousley ......6/3 7/6(4)
Julian Cash & Joshua Sapwell ......6/7(4) 6/4 6/4
Enzo Couacaud & Stefano Napolitano 6/4 6/4
Yoshihito Nishioka & Jorge Brian Panta [5] ...6/4 2/6 6/1
Maxime Janvier & Kamil Majchrzak 6/1 7/5
Thanasi Kokkinakis & Nick Kyrgios 4/6 6/3 6/4
Hugo Di Feo & Mazen Osama ...6/7(1) 7/6(7) 6/3
Johannes Haerteis & Hannes Wagner ......6/3 7/6(1)
Laslo Djere & Martin Redlicki ......7/6(7) 6/2
Filippo Baldi & Matteo Donati ......6/7(4) 6/4 6/2
Maxime Hamou & Johan Sebastien Tatlot [2] ...6/3 3/6 6/3

Quarter-Finals:
Kyle Edmund & Frederico Ferreira Silva [1] 6/4 6/3
Clement Geens & Noah Rubin [6] 6/4 6/4
Jay Andrijic & Bradley Mousley ......6/3 7/6(2)
Enzo Couacaud & Stefano Napolitano ......7/6(3) 7/6(3)
Yoshihito Nishioka & Jorge Brian Panta [5] ...7/6(2) 7/6(3)
Thanasi Kokkinakis & Nick Kyrgios 6/2 6/3
Johannes Haerteis & Hannes Wagner 6/3 6/3
Filippo Baldi & Matteo Donati 6/4 6/2

Semi-Finals:
Kyle Edmund & Frederico Ferreira Silva [1] ......7/6(3) 6/3
Enzo Couacaud & Stefano Napolitano 3/6 6/3 6/4
Thanasi Kokkinakis & Nick Kyrgios 6/3 6/2
Filippo Baldi & Matteo Donati ......6/3 7/6(5)

Final (left):
Enzo Couacaud & Stefano Napolitano ......6/4 7/6(7)
Thanasi Kokkinakis & Nick Kyrgios 6/4 3/6 6/2

Final:
Thanasi Kokkinakis & Nick Kyrgios 6/2 6/3

Heavy type denotes seeded players. The figure in brackets against names denotes the order in which they have been seeded. The Committee reserves the right to alter the seeding order in the event of withdrawals.
(WC) = Wild card. (Q) = Qualifier. (LL) = Lucky Loser.

EVENT VIII – THE GIRLS' SINGLES CHAMPIONSHIP 2013
Holder: EUGENIE BOUCHARD

The Champion will become the holder, for the year only, of a Cup presented by The All England Lawn Tennis and Croquet Club. The Champion will receive a three-quarter size Cup and the Runner-up will receive a Silver Salver. The matches will be best of three sets.

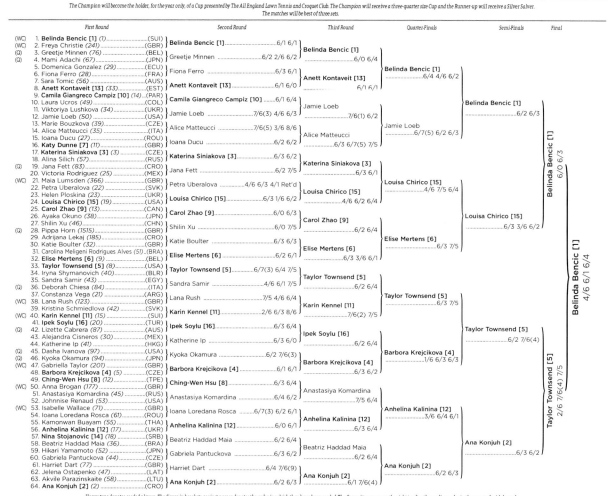

Heavy type denotes seeded players. The figure in brackets against names denotes the order in which they have been seeded. The Committee reserves the right to alter the seeding order in the event of withdrawals.
(WC) = Wild card. (Q) = Qualifier. (LL) = Lucky Loser.

EVENT IX – THE GIRLS' DOUBLES CHAMPIONSHIP 2013
Holders: EUGENIE BOUCHARD & TAYLOR TOWNSEND

The Champions will become the holders, for the year only, of a Cup presented by The All England Lawn Tennis and Croquet Club. The Champions will receive a three-quarter size Cup and the Runners-up will receive a Silver Salvers. The matches will be best of three sets.

Heavy type denotes seeded players. The figure in brackets against names denotes the order in which they have been seeded. The Committee reserves the right to alter the seeding order in the event of withdrawals.
(WC) = Wild card. (Q) = Qualifier. (LL) = Lucky Loser.

EVENT X – THE GENTLEMEN'S INVITATION DOUBLES 2013
Holders: GREG RUSEDSKI & FABRICE SANTORO

The Champions will become the holders, for the year only, of a Cup presented by The All England Lawn Tennis and Croquet Club. The Champions will receive a silver three-quarter size Cup. A Silver Medal will be presented to each of the Runners-up. The matches will be the best of three sets. If a match should reach one set all a 10 point tie-break will replace the third set.

GROUP A	Jonas Bjorkman (SWE) & Todd Woodbridge (AUS)	Justin Gimelstob (USA) & Todd Martin (USA)	Richard Krajicek (NED) & Mark Petchey (GBR)	Greg Rusedski (GBR) & Fabrice Santoro (FRA)	WINS	LOSSES
Jonas Bjorkman (SWE) & Todd Woodbridge (AUS)		6/3 2/6 [10-12] L	7/6(1) 6/2 W	3/6 6/7(4) L	1	2
Justin Gimelstob (USA) & Todd Martin (USA)	3/6 6/2 [12-10] W		6/1 6/4 W	1/6 6/4 [10-12] L	2	1
Richard Krajicek (NED) & Mark Petchey (GBR)	6/7(1) 2/6 L	1/6 4/6 L		W/O L	0	3
Greg Rusedski (GBR) & Fabrice Santoro (FRA)	6/3 7/6(4) W	6/1 4/6 [12-10] W	W/O W		3	0

GROUP B	Jacco Eltingh (NED) & Paul Haarhuis (NED)	Thomas Enqvist (SWE) & Mark Philippoussis (AUS)	Wayne Ferreira (RSA) & Chris Wilkinson (GBR)	Barry Cowan (GBR) & Cedric Pioline (FRA)	WINS	LOSSES
Jacco Eltingh (NED) & Paul Haarhuis (NED)		4/6 4/6 L	6/3 7/6(3) W	7/6(2) 6/2 W	2	1
Thomas Enqvist (SWE) & Mark Philippoussis (AUS)	6/4 6/4 W		6/4 6/4 W	6/4 6/4 W	3	0
Wayne Ferreira (RSA) & Chris Wilkinson (GBR)	3/6 6/7(3) L	4/6 4/6 L		4/6 2/6 L	0	3
Barry Cowan (GBR) & Cedric Pioline (FRA)	6/7(2) 2/6 L	4/6 4/6 L	6/4 6/2 W		1	2

FINAL: Greg Rusedski (GBR) & Fabrice Santoro (FRA) / Thomas Enqvist (SWE) & Mark Philippoussis (AUS) — Winner: Thomas Enqvist (SWE) & Mark Philippoussis (AUS) 7/6(6) 6/3

This event will be played on a 'round robin' basis. Eight invited pairs have been divided into two groups and each pair in each group will play one another. The pairs winning most matches will be the champions of their respective groups and will play each other in the final as indicated above. If matches should be equal in any group, the head-to-head result between the two pairs with the same number of wins will determine the winning pair of the group.

EVENT XI – THE GENTLEMEN'S SENIOR INVITATION DOUBLES 2013
Holders: PAT CASH & MARK WOODFORDE

The Champions will become the holders, for the year only, of a Cup presented by The All England Lawn Tennis and Croquet Club. The Champions will receive a silver half-size Cup. A Silver Medal will be presented to each of the Runners-up. The matches will be the best of three sets. If a match should reach one set all a 10 point tie-break will replace the third set.

GROUP A	Pat Cash (AUS) & Mark Woodforde (AUS)	Andrew Castle (GBR) & Guy Forget (FRA)	Peter Fleming (USA) & Johan Kriek (USA)	Joakim Nystrom (SWE) & Mikael Pernfors (SWE)	WINS	LOSSES
Pat Cash (AUS) & Mark Woodforde (AUS)		6/2 6/3 W	4/6 6/0 [10-8] W	6/2 0/0 Ret'd W	3	0
Andrew Castle (GBR) & Guy Forget (FRA)	2/6 3/6 L		6/3 6/4 W	4/6 2/6 L	1	2
Peter Fleming (USA) & Johan Kriek (USA)	6/4 0/6 [8-10] L	3/6 4/6 L		W/O W	1	2
Joakim Nystrom (SWE) & Mikael Pernfors (SWE)	2/6 0/0 Ret'd L	6/4 6/2 W	W/O L		1	2

GROUP B	Mansour Bahrami (IRI) & Henri Leconte (FRA)	Jeremy Bates (GBR) & Anders Jarryd (SWE)	John McEnroe (USA) & Patrick McEnroe (USA)	Peter McNamara (AUS) & Paul McNamee (AUS)	WINS	LOSSES
Mansour Bahrami (IRI) & Henri Leconte (FRA)		1/6 2/6 L	1/6 4/6 L	6/7(1) 4/6 L	0	3
Jeremy Bates (GBR) & Anders Jarryd (SWE)	6/1 6/2 W		7/5 5/7 [10-7] W	6/4 6/2 W	3	0
John McEnroe (USA) & Patrick McEnroe (USA)	6/1 6/4 W	5/7 7/5 [7-10] L		6/1 6/2 W	2	1
Peter McNamara (AUS) & Paul McNamee (AUS)	7/6(1) 6/4 W	4/6 2/6 L	1/6 2/6 L		1	2

FINAL: Pat Cash (AUS) & Mark Woodforde (AUS) / Jeremy Bates (GBR) & Anders Jarryd (SWE) — Winner: Pat Cash (AUS) & Mark Woodforde (AUS) 6/3 6/3

This event will be played on a 'round robin' basis. Eight invited pairs have been divided into two groups and each pair in each group will play one another. The pairs winning most matches will be the champions of their respective groups and will play each other in the final as indicated above. If matches should be equal in any group, the head-to-head result between the two pairs with the same number of wins will determine the winning pair of the group.

ALPHABETICAL LIST – INVITATION DOUBLES EVENTS
GENTLEMEN

Bjorkman, Jonas (Sweden)
Cowan, Barry (Great Britain)
Eltingh, Jacco (Netherlands)
Enqvist, Thomas (Sweden)
Ferreira, Wayne (South Africa)
Gimelstob, Justin (USA)
Haarhuis, Paul (Netherlands)
Krajicek, Richard (Netherlands)
Martin, Todd (USA)
Petchey, Mark (Great Britain)
Philippoussis, Mark (Australia)
Pioline, Cedric (France)
Rusedski, Greg (Great Britain)
Santoro, Fabrice (France)
Wilkinson, Chris (Great Britain)
Woodbridge, Todd (Australia)

LADIES

Ahl, Lucie (Great Britain)
Austin, Tracy (USA)
Davenport, Lindsay (USA)
Hingis, Martina (Switzerland)
Majoli, Iva (Croatia)
Maleeva, Magdalena (Bulgaria)
Martinez, Conchita (Spain)
Navratilova, Martina (USA)
Novotna, Jana (Czech Republic)
Schett, Barbara (Austria)
Shriver, Pam (USA)
Stubbs, Rennae (Australia)
Sukova, Helena (Czech Republic)
Tauziat, Nathalie (France)
Temesvari, Andrea (Hungary)
Zvereva, Natasha (Belarus)

ALPHABETICAL LIST – GENTLEMEN'S SENIOR INVITATION DOUBLES EVENTS

Bahrami, Mansour (Iran)
Bates, Jeremy (Great Britain)
Cash, Pat (Australia)
Castle, Andrew (Great Britain)
Fleming, Peter (USA)
Forget, Guy (France)
Jarryd, Anders (Sweden)
Kriek, Johan (USA)
Leconte, Henri (France)
McEnroe, John (USA)
McEnroe, Patrick (USA)
McNamara, Peter (Australia)
McNamee, Paul (Australia)
Nystrom, Joakim (Sweden)
Pernfors, Mikael (Sweden)
Woodforde, Mark (Australia)

EVENT XII – THE LADIES' INVITATION DOUBLES 2013
Holders: LINDSAY DAVENPORT & MARTINA HINGIS

The Champions will become the holders, for the year only, of a Cup presented by The All England Lawn Tennis and Croquet Club. The Champions will receive a silver three-quarter size Cup. A Silver Medal will be presented to each of the Runners-up. The matches will be the best of three sets. If a match should reach one set all a 10 point tie-break will replace the third set.

GROUP A	Tracy Austin (USA) & Helena Sukova (CZE)	Lindsay Davenport (USA) & Martina Hingis (SUI)	Conchita Martinez (ESP) & Nathalie Tauziat (FRA)	Rennae Stubbs (AUS) & Andrea Temesvari (HUN)	WINS	LOSSES	FINAL
Tracy Austin (USA) & Helena Sukova (CZE)		2/6 5/7 L	6/1 6/1 W	6/4 6/2 W	2	1	
Lindsay Davenport (USA) & Martina Hingis (SUI)	6/2 7/5 W		6/3 6/1 W	7/5 6/2 W	3	0	Lindsay Davenport (USA) & Martina Hingis (SUI)
Conchita Martinez (ESP) & Nathalie Tauziat (FRA)	1/6 1/6 L	3/6 1/6 L		4/6 3/6 L	0	3	
Rennae Stubbs (AUS) & Andrea Temesvari (HUN)	4/6 2/6 L	5/7 2/6 L	6/4 6/3 W		1	2	

Final: Lindsay Davenport (USA) & Martina Hingis (SUI) 6/2 6/2

GROUP B	Lucie Ahl (GBR) & Magdalena Maleeva (BUL)	Iva Majoli (CRO) & Natasha Zvereva (BLR)	Martina Navratilova (USA) & Pam Shriver (USA)	Jana Novotna (CZE) & Barbara Schett (AUT)	WINS	LOSSES	FINAL
Lucie Ahl (GBR) & Magdalena Maleeva (BUL)		6/0 5/7 [10-8] W	6/2 7/6(6) W	2/6 7/6(2) [2-10] L	2	1	
Iva Majoli (CRO) & Natasha Zvereva (BLR)	0/6 7/5 [8-10] L		6/2 6/3 W	3/6 3/6 L	1	2	
Martina Navratilova (USA) & Pam Shriver (USA)	2/6 6/7(6) L	2/6 3/6 L		1/6 4/6 L	0	3	Jana Novotna (CZE) & Barbara Schett (AUT)
Jana Novotna (CZE) & Barbara Schett (AUT)	6/2 6/7(2) [10-2] W	6/3 6/3 W	6/1 6/4 W		3	0	

This event will be played on a 'round robin' basis. Eight invited pairs have been divided into two groups of four and each pair in each group will play one another. The pairs winning most matches will be the champions of their respective groups and will play each other in the final as indicated above. If matches should be equal in any group, the head-to-head result between the two pairs with the same number of wins will determine the winning pair of the group.

EVENT XIII – THE WHEELCHAIR GENTLEMEN'S DOUBLES 2013
Holders: TOM EGBERINK & MICHAEL JEREMIASZ

The Champions will receive Silver Salvers. The matches will be the best of three tie-break sets.

Third & Fourth Place Play-off

Gordon Reid & Maikel Scheffers

Tom Egberink & Michael Jeremiasz

Tom Egberink & Michael Jeremiasz 6/4 6/3

First Round

1. **Stephane Houdet** (FRA) & **Shingo Kunieda** (JPN) .... **[1]**

2. Gordon Reid (GBR) & Maikel Scheffers (NED) ....

3. **Tom Egberink** (NED) & **Michael Jeremiasz** (FRA) .... (WC)

4. **Frederic Cattaneo** (FRA) & **Ronald Vink** (NED) .... **[2]**

Final

Stephane Houdet & Shingo Kunieda [1] 6/3 6/3

Frederic Cattaneo & Ronald Vink [2] 6/4 4/6 6/4

Stephane Houdet & Shingo Kunieda [1] 6/4 6/2

Heavy type denotes seeded players. The figure in brackets against names denotes the order in which they have been seeded.

EVENT XIV – THE WHEELCHAIR LADIES' DOUBLES 2013
Holders: JISKE GRIFFIOEN & ANIEK VAN KOOT

The Champions will receive Silver Salvers. The matches will be the best of three tie-break sets.

Third & Fourth Place Play-off

Sabine Ellerbrock & Sharon Walraven

Marjolein Buis & Lucy Shuker [2]

Marjolein Buis & Lucy Shuker [2] 7/5 7/6(6)

First Round

1. **Jiske Griffioen** (NED) & **Aniek Van Koot** (NED) .... **[1]**

2. Sabine Ellerbrock (GER) & Sharon Walraven (NED) ....

3. Yui Kamiji (JPN) & Jordanne Whiley (GBR) ....(WC)

4. **Marjolein Buis** (NED) & **Lucy Shuker** (GBR) .... **[2]**

Final

Jiske Griffioen & Aniek Van Koot [1] 6/3 6/2

Yui Kamiji & Jordanne Whiley 6/1 6/2

Jiske Griffioen & Aniek Van Koot [1] 6/4 7/6(6)

Heavy type denotes seeded players. The figure in brackets against names denotes the order in which they have been seeded.

ROLLS OF HONOUR
GENTLEMEN'S SINGLES CHAMPIONS & RUNNERS-UP

1877	S.W.Gore	1903	H.L.Doherty
	W.C.Marshall		F.L.Riseley
1878	P.F.Hadow	1904	H.L.Doherty
	S.W.Gore		F.L.Riseley
* 1879	J.T.Hartley	1905	H.L.Doherty
	V.St.L.Goold		N.E.Brookes
1880	J.T.Hartley	1906	H.L.Doherty
	H.F.Lawford		F.L.Riseley
1881	W.Renshaw	* 1907	N.E.Brookes
	J.T.Hartley		A.W.Gore
1882	W.Renshaw	* 1908	A.W.Gore
	J.E.Renshaw		H.R.Roper Barrett
1883	W.Renshaw	1909	A.W.Gore
	J.E.Renshaw		M.J.G.Ritchie
1884	W.Renshaw	1910	A.F.Wilding
	H.F.Lawford		A.W.Gore
1885	W.Renshaw	1911	A.F.Wilding
	H.F.Lawford		H.R.Roper Barrett
1886	W.Renshaw	1912	A.F.Wilding
	H.F.Lawford		A.W.Gore
* 1887	H.F.Lawford	1913	A.F.Wilding
	J.E.Renshaw		M.E.McLoughlin
1888	J.E.Renshaw	1914	N.E.Brookes
	H.F.Lawford		A.F.Wilding
1889	W.Renshaw	1919	G.L.Patterson
	J.E.Renshaw		N.E.Brookes
1890	W.J.Hamilton	1920	W.T.Tilden
	W.Renshaw		G.L.Patterson
* 1891	W.Baddeley	1921	W.T.Tilden
	J.Pim		B.I.C.Norton
1892	W.Baddeley	*† 1922	G.L.Patterson
	J.Pim		R.Lycett
1893	J.Pim	* 1923	W.M.Johnston
	W.Baddeley		F.T.Hunter
1894	J.Pim	* 1924	J.Borotra
	W.Baddeley		J.R.Lacoste
* 1895	W.Baddeley	1925	J.R.Lacoste
	W.V.Eaves		J.Borotra
1896	H.S.Mahony	* 1926	J.Borotra
	W.Baddeley		H.Kinsey
1897	R.F.Doherty	1927	H.Cochet
	H.S.Mahony		J.Borotra
1898	R.F.Doherty	1928	R.Lacoste
	H.L.Doherty		H.Cochet
1899	R.F.Doherty	* 1929	H.Cochet
	A.W.Gore		J.Borotra
1900	R.F.Doherty	1930	W.T.Tilden
	S.H.Smith		W.Allison
1901	A.W.Gore	* 1931	S.B.Wood
	R.F.Doherty		F.X.Shields
1902	H.L.Doherty	1932	H.E.Vines
	A.W.Gore		H.W.Austin

1933	J.H.Crawford	1965	R.Emerson
	H.E.Vines		F.S.Stolle
1934	F.J.Perry	1966	M.Santana
	J.H.Crawford		R.D.Ralston
1935	F.J.Perry	1967	J.D.Newcombe
	G.von Cramm		W.P.Bungert
1936	F.J.Perry	1968	R.Laver
	G.von Cramm		A.D.Roche
* 1937	J.D.Budge	1969	R.Laver
	G.von Cramm		J.D.Newcombe
1938	J.D.Budge	1970	J.D.Newcombe
	H.W.Austin		K.R.Rosewall
* 1939	R.L.Riggs	1971	J.D.Newcombe
	E.T.Cooke		S.R.Smith
* 1946	Y.Petra	* 1972	S.R.Smith
	G.E.Brown		I.Nastase
1947	J.Kramer	* 1973	J.Kodes
	T.Brown		A.Metreveli
* 1948	R.Falkenburg	1974	J.S.Connors
	J.E.Bromwich		K.R.Rosewall
1949	F.R.Schroeder	1975	A.R.Ashe
	J.Drobny		J.S.Connors
* 1950	B.Patty	1976	B.Borg
	F.A.Sedgman		I.Nastase
1951	R.Savitt	1977	B.Borg
	K.McGregor		J.S.Connors
1952	F.A.Sedgman	1978	B.Borg
	J.Drobny		J.S.Connors
* 1953	E.V.Seixas	1979	B.Borg
	K.Nielsen		L.R.Tanner
1954	J.Drobny	1980	B.Borg
	K.R.Rosewall		J.P.McEnroe
1955	T.Trabert	1981	J.P.McEnroe
	K.Nielsen		B.Borg
* 1956	L.A.Hoad	1982	J.S.Connors
	K.R.Rosewall		J.P.McEnroe
1957	L.A.Hoad	1983	J.P.McEnroe
	A.J.Cooper		C.J.Lewis
* 1958	A.J.Cooper	1984	J.P.McEnroe
	N.A.Fraser		J.S.Connors
* 1959	A.Olmedo	1985	B.Becker
	R.Laver		K.Curren
* 1960	N.A.Fraser	1986	B.Becker
	R.Laver		I.Lendl
1961	R.Laver	1987	P.Cash
	C.R.McKinley		I.Lendl
1962	R.Laver	1988	S.Edberg
	M.F.Mulligan		B.Becker
* 1963	C.R.McKinley	1989	B.Becker
	F.S.Stolle		S.Edberg
1964	R.Emerson	1990	S.Edberg
	F.S.Stolle		B.Becker

1991	M.Stich
	B.Becker
1992	A.Agassi
	G.Ivanisevic
1993	P.Sampras
	J.Courier
1994	P.Sampras
	G.Ivanisevic
1995	P.Sampras
	B.Becker
1996	R.Krajicek
	M.Washington
1997	P.Sampras
	C.Pioline
1998	P.Sampras
	G.Ivanisevic
1999	P.Sampras
	A.Agassi
2000	P.Sampras
	P.Rafter
2001	G.Ivanisevic
	P.Rafter
2002	L.Hewitt
	D.Nalbandian
2003	R.Federer
	M.Philippoussis
2004	R.Federer
	A.Roddick
2005	R.Federer
	A.Roddick
2006	R.Federer
	R.Nadal
2007	R.Federer
	R.Nadal
2008	R.Nadal
	R.Federer
2009	R.Federer
	A.Roddick
2010	R.Nadal
	T.Berdych
2011	N.Djokovic
	R.Nadal
2012	R.Federer
	A.Murray
2013	A.Murray
	N.Djokovic

For the years 1913, 1914 and 1919-1923 inclusive the above records include the "World's Championships on Grass" granted to The Lawn Tennis Association by The International Lawn Tennis Federation.
This title was then abolished and commencing in 1924 they became The Official Lawn Tennis Championships recognised by The International Lawn Tennis Federation.
Prior to 1922 the holders in the Singles Events and Gentlemen's Doubles did not compete in The Championships but met the winners of these events in the Challenge Rounds.
† Challenge Round abolished: holders subsequently played through.
* The holder did not defend the title.

LADIES' SINGLES CHAMPIONS & RUNNERS-UP

1884	Miss M.Watson	1910	Mrs.R.L.Chambers	*1946	Miss P.Betz
	Miss L.Watson		*Miss D.P.Boothby*		*Miss A.L.Brough*
1885	Miss M.Watson	1911	Mrs.R.L.Chambers	*1947	Miss M.Osborne
	Miss B.Bingley		*Miss D.P.Boothby*		*Miss D.Hart*
1886	Miss B.Bingley	*1912	Mrs.D.T.R.Larcombe	1948	Miss A.L.Brough
	Miss M.Watson		*Mrs.A.Sterry*		*Miss D.Hart*
1887	Miss C.Dod	*1913	Mrs.R.L.Chambers	1949	Miss A.L.Brough
	Miss B.Bingley		*Mrs.R.J.McNair*		*Mrs.W.du Pont*
1888	Miss C.Dod	1914	Mrs.R.L.Chambers	1950	Miss A.L.Brough
	Mrs.G.W.Hillyard		*Mrs.D.T.R.Larcombe*		*Mrs.W.du Pont*
*1889	Mrs.G.W.Hillyard	1919	Miss S.Lenglen	1951	Miss D.Hart
	Miss H.Rice		*Mrs.R.L.Chambers*		*Miss S.Fry*
*1890	Miss H.Rice	1920	Miss S.Lenglen	1952	Miss M.Connolly
	Miss M.Jacks		*Mrs.R.L.Chambers*		*Miss A.L.Brough*
*1891	Miss C.Dod	1921	Miss S.Lenglen	1953	Miss M.Connolly
	Mrs.G.W.Hillyard		*Miss E.Ryan*		*Miss D.Hart*
1892	Miss C.Dod	†1922	Miss S.Lenglen	1954	Miss M.Connolly
	Mrs.G.W.Hillyard		*Mrs.F.Mallory*		*Miss A.L.Brough*
1893	Miss C.Dod	1923	Miss S.Lenglen	*1955	Miss A.L.Brough
	Mrs.G.W.Hillyard		*Miss K.McKane*		*Mrs.J.G.Fleitz*
*1894	Mrs.G.W.Hillyard	1924	Miss K.McKane	1956	Miss S.Fry
	Miss E.L.Austin		*Miss H.Wills*		*Miss A.Buxton*
*1895	Miss C.Cooper	1925	Miss S.Lenglen	*1957	Miss A.Gibson
	Miss H.Jackson		*Miss J.Fry*		*Miss D.R.Hard*
1896	Miss C.Cooper	1926	Mrs.L.A.Godfree	1958	Miss A.Gibson
	Mrs.W.H.Pickering		*Miss E.M.de Alvarez*		*Miss F.A.Mortimer*
1897	Mrs.G.W.Hillyard	1927	Miss H.Wills	*1959	Miss M.E.Bueno
	Miss C.Cooper		*Miss E.M.de Alvarez*		*Miss D.R.Hard*
*1898	Miss C.Cooper	1928	Miss H.Wills	1960	Miss M.E.Bueno
	Miss L.Martin		*Miss E.M.de Alvarez*		*Miss S.Reynolds*
1899	Mrs.G.W.Hillyard	1929	Miss H.Wills	*1961	Miss F.A.Mortimer
	Miss C.Cooper		*Miss H.H.Jacobs*		*Miss C.C.Truman*
1900	Mrs.G.W.Hillyard	1930	Mrs.F.S.Moody	1962	Mrs.J.R.Susman
	Miss C.Cooper		*Miss E.Ryan*		*Mrs.C.Sukova*
1901	Mrs.A.Sterry	*1931	Miss C.Aussem	*1963	Miss M.Smith
	Mrs.G.W.Hillyard		*Miss H.Krahwinkel*		*Miss B.J.Moffitt*
1902	Miss M.E.Robb	*1932	Mrs.F.S.Moody	1964	Miss M.E.Bueno
	Mrs.A.Sterry		*Miss H.H.Jacobs*		*Miss M.Smith*
*1903	Miss D.K.Douglass	1933	Mrs.F.S.Moody	1965	Miss M.Smith
	Miss E.W.Thomson		*Miss D.E.Round*		*Miss M.E.Bueno*
1904	Miss D.K.Douglass	*1934	Miss D.E.Round	1966	Mrs.L.W.King
	Mrs.A.Sterry		*Miss H.H.Jacobs*		*Miss M.E.Bueno*
1905	Miss M.Sutton	1935	Mrs.F.S.Moody	1967	Mrs.L.W.King
	Miss D.K.Douglass		*Miss H.H.Jacobs*		*Mrs.P.F.Jones*
1906	Miss D.K.Douglass	*1936	Miss H.H.Jacobs	1968	Mrs.L.W.King
	Miss M.Sutton		*Miss S.Sperling*		*Miss J.A.M.Tegart*
1907	Miss M.Sutton	1937	Mrs.D.E.Round	1969	Mrs.P.F.Jones
	Mrs.R.L.Chambers		*Miss J.Jedrzejowska*		*Mrs.L.W.King*
*1908	Mrs.A.Sterry	*1938	Mrs.F.S.Moody	*1970	Mrs.B.M.Court
	Miss A.M.Morton		*Miss H.H.Jacobs*		*Mrs.L.W.King*
*1909	Miss D.P.Boothby	*1939	Miss A.Marble	1971	Miss E.F.Goolagong
	Miss A.M.Morton		*Miss K.E.Stammers*		*Mrs.B.M.Court*

1972	Mrs.L.W.King	*1997	Miss M.Hingis
	Miss E.F.Goolagong		*Miss J.Novotna*
1973	Mrs.L.W.King	1998	Miss J.Novotna
	Miss C.M.Evert		*Miss N.Tauziat*
1974	Miss C.M.Evert	1999	Miss L.A.Davenport
	Mrs.O.Morozova		*Miss S.Graf*
1975	Mrs.L.W.King	2000	Miss V.Williams
	Mrs.R.Cawley		*Miss L.A.Davenport*
*1976	Miss C.M.Evert	2001	Miss V.Williams
	Mrs.R.Cawley		*Miss J.Henin*
1977	Miss S.V.Wade	2002	Miss S.Williams
	Miss B.F.Stove		*Miss V.Williams*
1978	Miss M.Navratilova	2003	Miss S.Williams
	Miss C.M.Evert		*Miss V.Williams*
1979	Miss M.Navratilova	2004	Miss M.Sharapova
	Mrs.J.M.Lloyd		*Miss S.Williams*
1980	Mrs.R.Cawley	2005	Miss V.Williams
	Mrs.J.M.Lloyd		*Miss L.Davenport*
*1981	Mrs.J.M.Lloyd	2006	Miss A.Mauresmo
	Miss H.Mandlikova		*Mrs.J.Henin*
1982	Miss M.Navratilova		*Hardenne*
	Mrs.J.M.Lloyd	2007	Miss V.Williams
1983	Miss M.Navratilova		*Miss M.Bartoli*
	Miss A.Jaeger	2008	Miss V.Williams
1984	Miss M.Navratilova		*Miss S.Williams*
	Mrs.J.M.Lloyd	2009	Miss S.Williams
1985	Miss M.Navratilova		*Miss V.Williams*
	Mrs.J.M.Lloyd	2010	Miss S.Williams
1986	Miss M.Navratilova		*Miss V.Zvonareva*
	Miss H.Mandlikova	2011	Miss P.Kvitova
1987	Miss M.Navratilova		*Miss M.Sharapova*
	Miss S.Graf	2012	Miss S.Williams
1988	Miss S.Graf		*Miss A.Radwanska*
	Miss M.Navratilova	2013	Miss M.Bartoli
1989	Miss S.Graf		*Miss S.Lisicki*
	Miss M.Navratilova		
1990	Miss M.Navratilova		
	Miss Z.Garrison		
1991	Miss S.Graf		
	Miss G.Sabatini		
1992	Miss S.Graf		
	Miss M.Seles		
1993	Miss S.Graf		
	Miss J.Novotna		
1994	Miss C.Martinez		
	Miss M.Navratilova		
1995	Miss S.Graf		
	Miss A.Sanchez		
	Vicario		
1996	Miss S.Graf		
	Miss A.Sanchez		
	Vicario		

MAIDEN NAMES OF LADIES' CHAMPIONS (In the tables the following have been recorded in both married and single identities)

Mrs. R. Cawley	Miss E. F. Goolagong	Mrs. G. W. Hillyard	Miss B. Bingley	Mrs. G. E. Reid	Miss K. Melville
Mrs. R. L. Chambers	Miss D. K. Douglass	Mrs. P. F. Jones	Miss A. S. Haydon	Mrs. P. D. Smylie	Miss E. M. Sayers
Mrs. B. M. Court	Miss M. Smith	Mrs. L. W. King	Miss B. J. Moffitt	Frau S. Sperling	Fräulein H. Krahwinkel
Mrs. B. C. Covell	Miss P. L. Howkins	Mrs. M. R. King	Miss P. E. Mudford	Mrs. A. Sterry	Miss C. Cooper
Mrs. D. E. Dalton	Miss J. A. M. Tegart	Mrs. D. T. R. Larcombe	Miss E. W. Thomson	Mrs. J. R. Susman	Miss K. Hantze
Mrs. W. du Pont	Miss M. Osborne	Mrs. J. M. Lloyd	Miss C. M. Evert		
Mrs. L. A. Godfree	Miss K. McKane	Mrs. F. S. Moody	Miss H. Wills		
Mrs. H. F. Gourlay Cawley	Miss H. F. Gourlay	Mrs. O. Morozova	Miss O. Morozova		
Mrs. J. Henin-Hardenne	Miss J. Henin	Mrs. L. E. G. Price	Miss S. Reynolds		

GENTLEMEN'S DOUBLES CHAMPIONS & RUNNERS-UP

1879 L.R.Erskine and H.F.Lawford
F.Durant and G.E.Tabor

1880 W.Renshaw and J.E.Renshaw
O.E.Woodhouse and C.J.Cole

1881 W.Renshaw and J.E.Renshaw
W.J.Down and H.Vaughan

1882 J.T.Hartley and R.T.Richardson
J.G.Horn and C.B.Russell

1883 C.W.Grinstead and C.E.Welldon
C.B.Russell and R.T.Milford

1884 W.Renshaw and J.E.Renshaw
E.W.Lewis and E.L.Williams

1885 W.Renshaw and J.E.Renshaw
C.E.Farrer and A.J.Stanley

1886 W.Renshaw and J.E.Renshaw
C.E.Farrer and A.J.Stanley

1887 P.Bowes-Lyon and H.W.W.Wilberforce
J.H.Crispe and E.Barratt Smith

1888 W.Renshaw and J.E.Renshaw
P.Bowes-Lyon and H.W.W.Wilberforce

1889 W.Renshaw and J.E.Renshaw
E.W.Lewis and G.W.Hillyard

1890 J.Pim and F.O.Stoker
E.W.Lewis and G.W.Hillyard

1891 W.Baddeley and H.Baddeley
J.Pim and F.O.Stoker

1892 H.S.Barlow and E.W.Lewis
W.Baddeley and H.Baddeley

1893 J.Pim and F.O.Stoker
E.W.Lewis and H.S.Barlow

1894 W.Baddeley and H.Baddeley
H.S.Barlow and C.H.Martin

1895 W.Baddeley and H.Baddeley
E.W.Lewis and W.V.Eaves

1896 W.Baddeley and H.Baddeley
R.F.Doherty and H.A.Nisbet

1897 R.F.Doherty and H.L.Doherty
W.Baddeley and H.Baddeley

1898 R.F.Doherty and H.L .Doherty
H.A.Nisbet and C.Hobart

1899 R.F.Doherty and H.L.Doherty
H.A.Nisbet and C.Hobart

1900 R.F.Doherty and H.L.Doherty
H.R.Roper Barrett and H.A.Nisbet

1901 R.F.Doherty and H.L.Doherty
D.Davis and H.Ward

1902 S.H.Smith and F.L.Riseley
R.F.Doherty and H.L.Doherty

1903 R.F.Doherty and H.L.Doherty
S.H.Smith and F.L.Riseley

1904 R.F.Doherty and H.L.Doherty
S.H.Smith and F.L.Riseley

1905 R.F.Doherty and H.L.Doherty
S.H.Smith and F.L.Riseley

1906 S.H.Smith and F.L.Riseley
R.F.Doherty and H.L.Doherty

1907 N.E.Brookes and A.F.Wilding
B.C.Wright and K.H.Behr

1908 A.F.Wilding and M.J.G.Ritchie
A.W.Gore and H.R.Roper Barrett

1909 A.W.Gore and H.R.Roper Barrett
S.N.Doust and H.A.Parker

1910 A.F.Wilding and M.J.G.Ritchie
A.W.Gore and H.R.Roper Barrett

1911 M.Decugis and A.H.Gobert
M.J.G.Ritchie and A.F.Wilding

1912 H.R.Roper Barrett and C.P.Dixon
M.Decugis and A.H.Gobert

1913 H.R.Roper Barrett and C.P.Dixon
F.W.Rahe and H.Kleinschroth

1914 N.E.Brookes and A.F.Wilding
H.R.Roper Barrett and C.P.Dixon

1919 R.V.Thomas and P.O.Wood
R.Lycett and R.W.Heath

1920 R.N.Williams and C.S.Garland
A.R.F.Kingscote and J.C.Parke

1921 R.Lycett and M.Woosnam
F.G.Lowe and A.H.Lowe

1922 R.Lycett and J.O.Anderson
G.L.Patterson and P.O.Wood

1923 R.Lycett and L.A.Godfree
Count de Gomar and E.Flaquer

1924 F.T.Hunter and V.Richards
R.N.Williams and W.M.Washburn

1925 J.Borotra and R.Lacoste
J.Hennessey and R.Casey

1926 H.Cochet and J.Brugnon
V.Richards and H.Kinsey

1927 F.T.Hunter and W.T.Tilden
J.Brugnon and H.Cochet

1928 H.Cochet and J.Brugnon
G.L.Patterson and J.B.Hawkes

1929 W.Allison and J.Van Ryn
J.C.Gregory and I.G.Collins

1930 W.Allison and J.Van Ryn
J.H.Doeg and G.M.Lott

1931 G.M Lott and J.Van Ryn
H.Cochet and J.Brugnon

1932 J.Borotra and J.Brugnon
G.P.Hughes and F.J.Perry

1933 J.Borotra and J.Brugnon
R.Nunoi and J.Satoh

1934 G.M.Lott and L.R.Stoefen
J.Borotra and J.Brugnon

1935 J.H.Crawford and A.K.Quist
W.Allison and J.Van Ryn

1936 G.P.Hughes and C.R.D.Tuckey
C.E.Hare and F.H.D.Wilde

1937 J.D.Budge and G.C.Mako
G.P.Hughes and C.R.D.Tuckey

1938 J.D.Budge and G.C.Mako
H.Henkel and G.von Metaxa

1939 R.L.Riggs and E.T.Cooke
C.E.Hare and F.H.D.Wilde

1946 T.Brown and J.Kramer
G.E.Brown and D.Pails

1947 R.Falkenburg and J.Kramer
A.J.Mottram and O.W.Sidwell

1948 J.E.Bromwich and F.A.Sedgman
T.Brown and G.Mulloy

1949 R.Gonzales and F.Parker
G.Mulloy and F.R.Schroeder

1950 J.E.Bromwich and A.K.Quist
G.E.Brown and O.W Sidwell

1951 K.McGregor and F.A.Sedgman
J.Drobny and E.W.Sturgess

1952 K.McGregor and F.A.Sedgman
E.V.Seixas and E.W.Sturgess

1953 L.A.Hoad and K.R.Rosewall
R.N.Hartwig and M.G.Rose

1954 R.N.Hartwig and M.G.Rose
E.V.Seixas and T.Trabert

1955 R.N.Hartwig and L.A.Hoad
N.A.Fraser and K.R.Rosewall

1956 L.A.Hoad and K.R.Rosewall
N.Pietrangeli and O.Sirola

1957 G.Mulloy and B.Patty
N.A.Fraser and L.A.Hoad

1958 S.Davidson and U.Schmidt
A.J.Cooper and N.A.Fraser

1959 R.Emerson and N.A.Fraser
R.Laver and R.Mark

1960 R.H.Osuna and R.D.Ralston
M.G.Davies and R.K.Wilson

1961 R.Emerson and N.A.Fraser
R.A.J.Hewitt and F.S.Stolle

1962 R.A.J.Hewitt and F.S.Stolle
B.Jovanovic and N.Pilic

1963 R.H.Osuna and A.Palafox
J.C.Barclay and P.Darmon

1964 R.A.J.Hewitt and F.S.Stolle
R.Emerson and K.N.Fletcher

1965 J.D.Newcombe and A.D.Roche
K.N.Fletcher and R.A.J.Hewitt

1966 K.N.Fletcher and J.D.Newcombe
W.W.Bowrey and O.K.Davidson

1967 R.A.J.Hewitt and F.D.McMillan
R.Emerson and K.N.Fletcher

1968 J.D.Newcombe and A.D.Roche
K.R.Rosewall and F.S.Stolle

1969 J.D.Newcombe and A.D.Roche
T.S.Okker and M.C.Reissen

1970 J.D.Newcombe and A.D.Roche
K.R.Rosewall and F.S.Stolle

1971 R.S.Emerson and R.G.Laver
A.R.Ashe and R.D.Ralston

1972 R.A.J.Hewitt and F.D.McMillan
S.R.Smith and E.J.van Dillen

1973 J.S.Connors and I.Nastase
J.R.Cooper and N.A.Fraser

1974 J.D.Newcombe and A.D.Roche
R.C.Lutz and S.R.Smith

1975 V.Gerulaitis and A.Mayer
C.Dowdeswell and A.J.Stone

1976 B.E.Gottfried and R.Ramirez
R.L.Case and G.Masters

1977 R.L.Case and G.Masters
J.G.Alexander and P.C.Dent

1978 R.A.J.Hewitt and F.D.McMillan
P.Fleming and J.P.McEnroe

1979 P.Fleming and J.P .McEnroe
B.E.Gottfried and R.Ramirez

1980 P.McNamara and P.McNamee
R.C.Lutz and S.R.Smith

1981 P.Fleming and J.P.McEnroe
R.C.Lutz and S.R.Smith

1982 P.McNamara and P.McNamee
P.Fleming and J.P.McEnroe

1983 P.Fleming and J.P McEnroe
T.E.Gullikson and T.R.Gullikson

1984 P.Fleming and J.P.McEnroe
P.Cash and P.McNamee

1985 H.P.Guenthardt and B.Taroczy
P.Cash and J.B.Fitzgerald

1986 J.Nystrom and M.Wilander
G.Donnelly and P.Fleming

1987 K.Flach and R.Seguso
S.Casal and E.Sanchez

1988 K.Flach and R.Seguso
J.B.Fitzgerald and A.Jarryd

1989 J.B.Fitzgerald and A.Jarryd
R.Leach and J.Pugh

1990 R.Leach and J.Pugh
P.Aldrich and D.T.Visser

1991 J.B.Fitzgerald and A.Jarryd
J.Frana and L.Lavalle

1992 J.P.McEnroe and M.Stich
J.Grabb and R.A.Reneberg

1993 T.A.Woodbridge and M.Woodforde
G.Connell and P.Galbraith

1994 T.A.Woodbridge and M.Woodforde
G.Connell and P.Galbraith

1995 T.A.Woodbridge and M.Woodforde
R.Leach and S.D.Melville

1996 T.A.Woodbridge and M.Woodforde
B.Black and G.Connell

1997 T.A.Woodbridge and M.Woodforde
J.Eltingh and P.Haarhuis

1998 J.Eltingh and P.Haarhuis
T.A.Woodbridge and M.Woodforde

1999 M.Bhupathi and L.Paes
P.Haarhuis and J.Palmer

2000 T.A.Woodbridge and M.Woodforde
P.Haarhuis and S.Stolle

2001 D.Johnson and J.Palmer
J.Novak and D.Rikl

2002 J.Bjorkman and T.A Woodbridge
M.Knowles and D.Nestor

2003 J.Bjorkman and T.A Woodbridge
M.Bhupathi and M.Mirnyi

2004 J.Bjorkman and T.A Woodbridge
J.Knowle and N.Zimonjic

2005 S.Huss and W.Moodie
R.Bryan and M.Bryan

2006 R.Bryan and M.Bryan
F.Santoro and N.Zimonjic

2007 A.Clement and M.Llodra
R.Bryan and M.Bryan

2008 D.Nestor and N.Zimonjic
J.Bjorkman and K.Ullyett

2009 D.Nestor and N.Zimonjic
R.Bryan and M.Bryan

2010 J.Melzer and P.Petzschner
R.Lindstedt and H.Tecau

2011 R.Bryan and M.Bryan
R.Linstedt and H.Tecau

2012 J.Marray and F.Nielsen
R.Linstedt and H.Tecau

2013 R.Bryan and M.Bryan
I.Dodig and M.Melo

LADIES' DOUBLES CHAMPIONS & RUNNERS-UP

1913	Mrs.R.J.McNair and Miss D.P.Boothby *Mrs.A.Sterry and Mrs.R.L.Chambers*	
1914	Miss E.Ryan and Miss A.M.Morton *Mrs.D.T.R.Larcombe and Mrs.F.J.Hannam*	
1919	Miss S.Lenglen and Miss E.Ryan *Mrs.R.L.Chambers and Mrs.D.T.R.Larcombe*	
1920	Miss S.Lenglen and Miss E.Ryan *Mrs.R.L.Chambers and Mrs.D.T.R.Larcombe*	
1921	Miss S.Lenglen and Miss E.Ryan *Mrs.A.E.Beamish and Mrs.G.E.Peacock*	
1922	Miss S.Lenglen and Miss E.Ryan *Mrs.A.D.Stocks and Miss K.McKane*	
1923	Miss S.Lenglen and Miss E.Ryan *Miss J.Austin and Miss E.L.Colyer*	
1924	Mrs.G.Wightman and Miss H.Wills *Mrs.B.C.Covell and Miss K.McKane*	
1925	Miss S.Lenglen and Miss E.Ryan *Mrs.A.V.Bridge and Mrs.C.G.McIlquham*	
1926	Miss E.Ryan and Miss M.K.Browne *Mrs.L.A.Godfree and Miss E.L.Colyer*	
1927	Miss H.Wills and Miss E.Ryan *Miss E.L.Heine and Mrs.G.E.Peacock*	
1928	Mrs.M.R.Watson and Miss M.A.Saunders *Miss E.H.Harvey and Miss E.Bennett*	
1929	Mrs.M.R.Watson and Mrs.L.R.C.Michell *Mrs.B.C.Covell and Mrs.W.P.Barron*	
1930	Mrs.F.S.Moody and Miss E.Ryan *Miss E.Cross and Miss S.Palfrey*	
1931	Mrs.W.P.Barron and Miss P.E.Mudford *Miss D.Metaxa and Miss J.Sigart*	
1932	Miss D.Metaxa and Miss J.Sigart *Miss E.Ryan and Miss H.H.Jacobs*	
1933	Mrs.R.Mathieu and Miss E.Ryan *Miss W.A.James and Miss A.M.Yorke*	
1934	Mrs.R.Mathieu and Miss E.Ryan *Mrs.D.Andrus and Mrs.C.F.Henrotin*	
1935	Miss W.A.James and Miss K.E.Stammers *Mrs.R.Mathieu and Mrs.S.Sperling*	
1936	Miss W.A.James and Miss K.E.Stammers *Mrs.M.Fabyan and Miss H.H.Jacobs*	
1937	Mrs.R.Mathieu and Miss A.M.Yorke *Mrs.M.R.King and Mrs.J.B.Pittman*	
1938	Mrs.M.Fabyan and Miss A.Marble *Mrs.R.Mathieu and Miss A.M.Yorke*	
1939	Mrs.M.Fabyan and Miss A.Marble *Miss H.H.Jacobs and Miss A.M.Yorke*	
1946	Miss A.L.Brough and Miss M.Osborne *Miss P.Betz and Miss D.Hart*	
1947	Miss D.Hart and Mrs.R.B.Todd *Miss A.L.Brough and Miss M.Osborne*	
1948	Miss A.L.Brough and Mrs.W.du Pont *Miss D.Hart and Mrs.R.B.Todd*	
1949	Miss A.L.Brough and Mrs.W.du Pont *Miss G.Moran and Mrs.R.B.Todd*	
1950	Miss A.L.Brough and Mrs.W.du Pont *Miss S.Fry and Miss D.Hart*	
1951	Miss S.Fry and Miss D.Hart *Miss A.L.Brough and Mrs.W.du Pont*	
1952	Miss S.Fry and Miss D.Hart *Miss A.L.Brough and Miss M.Connolly*	
1953	Miss S.Fry and Miss D.Hart *Miss M.Connolly and Miss J.Sampson*	
1954	Miss A.L.Brough and Mrs.W.du Pont *Miss S.Fry and Miss D.Hart*	
1955	Miss F.A.Mortimer and Miss J.A.Shilcock *Miss S.J.Bloomer and Miss P.E.Ward*	
1956	Miss A.Buxton and Miss A.Gibson *Miss F.Muller and Miss D.G.Seeney*	
1957	Miss A.Gibson and Miss D.R.Hard *Mrs.K.Hawton and Mrs.T.D.Long*	
1958	Miss M.E.Bueno and Miss A.Gibson *Mrs.W.du Pont and Miss M.Varner*	
1959	Miss J.Arth and Miss D.R.Hard *Mrs.J.G.Fleitz and Miss C.C.Truman*	
1960	Miss M.E.Bueno and Miss D.R.Hard *Miss S.Reynolds and Miss R.Schuurman*	
1961	Miss K.Hantze and Miss B.J.Moffitt *Miss J.Lehane and Miss M.Smith*	
1962	Miss B.J.Moffitt and Mrs.J.R.Susman *Mrs.L.E.G.Price and Miss R.Schuurman*	
1963	Miss M.E.Bueno and Miss D.R.Hard *Miss R.A.Ebbern and Miss M.Smith*	
1964	Miss M.Smith and Miss L.R.Turner *Miss B.J.Moffitt and Mrs.J.R.Susman*	
1965	Miss M.E.Bueno and Miss B.J.Moffitt *Miss F.Durr and Miss J.Lieffrig*	
1966	Miss M.E.Bueno and Miss N.Richey *Miss M.Smith and Miss J.A.M.Tegart*	
1967	Miss R.Casals and Mrs.L.W.King *Miss M.E.Bueno and Miss N.Richey*	
1968	Miss R.Casals and Mrs.L.W.King *Miss F.Durr and Mrs.P.F.Jones*	
1969	Mrs.B.M.Court and Miss J.A.M.Tegart *Miss P.S.A.Hogan and Miss M.Michel*	
1970	Miss R.Casals and Mrs.L.W.King *Miss F.Durr and Miss S.V.Wade*	
1971	Miss R.Casals and Mrs.L.W.King *Mrs.B.M.Court and Miss E.F.Goolagong*	
1972	Mrs.L.W.King and Miss B.F.Stove *Mrs.D.E.Dalton and Miss F.Durr*	
1973	Miss R.Casals and Mrs.L.W.King *Miss F.Durr and Miss B.F.Stove*	
1974	Miss E.F.Goolagong and Miss M.Michel *Miss H.F.Gourlay and Miss K.M.Krantzcke*	
1975	Miss A.Kiyomura and Miss K.Sawamatsu *Miss F.Durr and Miss B.F.Stove*	
1976	Miss C.M.Evert and Miss M.Navratilova *Mrs.L.W.King and Miss B.F.Stove*	
1977	Mrs.R.L.Cawley and Miss J.C.Russell *Miss M.Navratilova and Miss B.F.Stove*	
1978	Mrs.G.E.Reid and Miss W.M.Turnbull *Miss M.Jausovec and Miss V.Ruzici*	
1979	Mrs.L.W.King and Miss M.Navratilova *Miss B.F.Stove and Miss W.M.Turnbull*	
1980	Miss K.Jordan and Miss A.E.Smith *Miss R.Casals and Miss W.M.Turnbull*	
1981	Miss M.Navratilova and Miss P.H.Shriver *Miss K.Jordan and Miss A.E.Smith*	
1982	Miss M.Navratilova and Miss P.H.Shriver *Miss K.Jordan and Miss A.E.Smith*	
1983	Miss M.Navratilova and Miss P.H.Shriver *Miss R.Casals and Miss W.M.Turnbull*	
1984	Miss M.Navratilova and Miss P.H.Shriver *Miss K.Jordan and Miss A.E.Smith*	
1985	Miss K.Jordan and Mrs.P.D.Smylie *Miss M.Navratilova and Miss P.H.Shriver*	
1986	Miss M.Navratilova and Miss P.H.Shriver *Miss H.Mandlikova and Miss W.M.Turnbull*	
1987	Miss C.Kohde-Kilsch and Miss H.Sukova *Miss H.E.Nagelsen and Mrs.P.D.Smylie*	
1988	Miss S.Graf and Miss G.Sabatini *Miss L.Savchenko and Miss N.Zvereva*	
1989	Miss J.Novotna and Miss H.Sukova *Miss L.Savchenko and Miss N.Zvereva*	
1990	Miss J.Novotna and Miss H.Sukova *Miss K.Jordan and Mrs.P.D.Smylie*	
1991	Miss L.Savchenko and Miss N.Zvereva *Miss B.C.Fernandez and Miss J.Novotna*	
1992	Miss B.C.Fernandez and Miss N.Zvereva *Miss J.Novotna and Mrs.A.Neiland*	
1993	Miss B.C.Fernandez and Miss N.Zvereva *Mrs.A.Neiland and Miss J.Novotna*	
1994	Miss B.C.Fernandez and Miss N.Zvereva *Miss J.Novotna and Miss A.Sanchez Vicario*	
1995	Miss J.Novotna and Miss A.Sanchez Vicario *Miss B.C.Fernandez and Miss N.Zvereva*	
1996	Miss M.Hingis and Miss H.Sukova *Miss M.J.McGrath and Mrs.A.Neiland*	
1997	Miss B.C.Fernandez and Miss N.Zvereva *Miss N.J.Arendt and Miss M.M.Bollegraf*	
1998	Miss M.Hingis and Miss J.Novotna *Miss L.A.Davenport and Miss N.Zvereva*	
1999	Miss L.A.Davenport and Miss C.Morariu *Miss M.de Swardt and Miss E.Tatarkova*	
2000	Miss S.Williams and Miss V.Williams *Mrs.A.Decugis and Miss A.Sugiyama*	
2001	Miss L.M.Raymond and Miss R.P.Stubbs *Miss K.Clijsters and Miss A.Sugiyama*	
2002	Miss S.Williams and Miss V.Williams *Miss V.Ruano Pascual and Miss P.Suarez*	
2003	Miss K.Clijsters and Miss A.Sugiyama *Miss V.Ruano Pascual and Miss P.Suarez*	
2004	Miss C.Black and Miss R.P.Stubbs *Mrs.A.Huber and Miss A.Sugiyama*	
2005	Miss C.Black and Mrs.A.Huber *Miss S.Kuznetsova and Miss A.Muresmo*	
2006	Miss Z.Yan and Miss J.Zheng *Miss V.Ruano Pascual and Miss P.Suarez*	
2007	Miss C.Black and Mrs.A.Huber *Miss K.Srebotnik and Miss A.Sugiyama*	
2008	Miss S.Williams and Miss V.Williams *Miss L.M.Raymond and Miss S.Stosur*	
2009	Miss S.Williams and Miss V.Williams *Miss S.Stosur and Miss R.P.Stubbs*	
2010	Miss V.King and Miss Y.Shvedova *Miss E.Vesnina and Miss V.Zvonareva*	
2011	Miss K.Peschke and Miss K.Srebotnik *Miss S.Lisicki and Miss S.Stosur*	
2012	Miss S.Williams and Miss V.Williams *Miss A.Hlavackova and Miss L.Hradecka*	
2013	Miss S-W.Hsieh and Miss S.Peng *Miss A.Barty and Miss C.Dellacqua*	

MIXED DOUBLES CHAMPIONS & RUNNERS-UP

1913 H.Crisp and Mrs.C.O.Tuckey
J.C.Parke and Mrs.D.T.R.Larcombe

1914 J.C.Parke and Mrs.D.T.R.Larcombe
A.F.Wilding and Miss M.Broquedis

1919 R.Lycett and Miss E.Ryan
A.D.Prebble and Mrs.R.L.Chambers

1920 G.L.Patterson and Miss S.Lenglen
R.Lycett and Miss E.Ryan

1921 R.Lycett and Miss E.Ryan
M.Woosnam and Miss P.L.Howkins

1922 P.O.Wood and Miss S.Lenglen
R.Lycett and Miss E.Ryan

1923 R.Lycett and Miss E.Ryan
L.S.Deane and Mrs.W.P.Barron

1924 J.B.Gilbert and Miss K.McKane
L.A.Godfree and Mrs.W.P.Barron

1925 J.Borotra and Miss S.Lenglen
U.L.de Morpurgo and Miss E.Ryan

1926 L.A.Godfree and Mrs.L.A.Godfree
H.Kinsey and Miss M.K.Browne

1927 F.T.Hunter and Miss E.Ryan
L.A.Godfree and Mrs.L.A.Godfree

1928 P.D.B.Spence and Miss E.Ryan
J.Crawford and Miss D.Akhurst

1929 F.T.Hunter and Miss H.Wills
I.G.Collins and Miss J.Fry

1930 J.H.Crawford and Miss E.Ryan
D.Prenn and Miss H.Krahwinkel

1931 G.M.Lott and Mrs.L.A.Harper
I.G.Collins and Miss J.C.Ridley

1932 E.Maier and Miss E.Ryan
H.C.Hopman and Miss J.Sigart

1933 G.von Cramm and Miss H.Krahwinkel
N.G.Farquharson and Miss G.M.Heeley

1934 R.Miki and Miss D.E.Round
H.W.Austin and Mrs.W.P.Barron

1935 F.J.Perry and Miss D.E.Round
H.C.Hopman and Mrs.H.C.Hopman

1936 F.J.Perry and Miss D.E.Round
J.D.Budge and Mrs.M.Fabyan

1937 J.D.Budge and Miss A.Marble
Y.Petra and Mrs.R.Mathieu

1938 J.D.Budge and Miss A.Marble
H.Henkel and Mrs.M.Fabyan

1939 R.L.Riggs and Miss A.Marble
F.H.D.Wilde and Miss N.B.Brown

1946 T.Brown and Miss A.L.Brough
G.E.Brown and Miss D.Bundy

1947 J.E.Bromwich and Miss A.L.Brough
C.F.Long and Mrs.G.F.Bolton

1948 J.E.Bromwich and Miss A.L.Brough
F.A.Sedgman and Miss D.Hart

1949 E.W.Sturgess and Mrs.R.A.Summers
J.E.Bromwich and Miss A.L.Brough

1950 E.W.Sturgess and Miss A.L.Brough
G.E.Brown and Mrs.R.B.Todd

1951 F.A.Sedgman and Miss D.Hart
M.G.Rose and Mrs.G.F.Bolton

1952 F.A.Sedgman and Miss D.Hart
E.Morea and Mrs.M.N.Long

1953 E.V.Seixas and Miss D.Hart
E.Morea and Miss S.Fry

1954 E.V.Seixas and Miss D.Hart
K.R.Rosewall and Mrs.W.du Pont

1955 E.V.Seixas and Miss D.Hart
E.Morea and Miss A.L.Brough

1956 E.V.Seixas and Miss S.Fry
G.Mulloy and Miss A.Gibson

1957 M.G.Rose and Miss D.R.Hard
N.A.Fraser and Miss A.Gibson

1958 R.N.Howe and Miss L.Coghlan
K.Nielsen and Miss A.Gibson

1959 R.Laver and Miss D.R.Hard
N.A.Fraser and Miss M.E.Bueno

1960 R.Laver and Miss D.R.Hard
R.N.Howe and Miss M.E.Bueno

1961 F.S.Stolle and Miss L.R.Turner
R.N.Howe and Miss E.Buding

1962 N.A.Fraser and Mrs.W.du Pont
R.D.Ralston and Miss A.S.Haydon

1963 K.N.Fletcher and Miss M.Smith
R.A.J.Hewitt and Miss D.R.Hard

1964 F.S.Stolle and Miss L.R.Turner
K.N.Fletcher and Miss M.Smith

1965 K.N.Fletcher and Miss M.Smith
A.D.Roche and Miss J.A.M.Tegart

1966 K.N.Fletcher and Miss M.Smith
R.D.Ralston amd Mrs.L.W.King

1967 O.K.Davidson and Mrs.L.W.King
K.N.Fletcher and Miss M.E.Bueno

1968 K.N.Fletcher and Mrs.B.M.Court
A.Metreveli and Miss O.Morozova

1969 F.S.Stolle and Mrs.P.F.Jones
A.D.Roche and Miss J.A.M.Tegart

1970 I.Nastase and Miss R.Casals
A.Metreveli and Miss O.Morozova

1971 O.K.Davidson and Mrs.L.W.King
M.C.Riessen and Mrs.B.M.Court

1972 I.Nastase and Miss R.Casals
K.G.Warwick and Miss E.F.Goolagong

1973 O.K.Davidson and Mrs.L.W.King
R.Ramirez and Miss J.S.Newberry

1974 O.K.Davidson and Mrs.L.W.King
M.J.Farrell and Miss L.J.Charles

1975 M.C.Riessen and Mrs.B.M.Court
A.J.Stone and Miss B.F.Stove

1976 A.D.Roche and Miss F.Durr
R.L.Stockton and Miss R.Casals

1977 R.A.J.Hewitt and Miss G.R.Stevens
F.D.McMillan and Miss B.F.Stove

1978 F.D.McMillan and Miss B.F.Stove
R.O.Ruffels and Mrs.L.W.King

1979 R.A.J.Hewitt and Miss G.R.Stevens
F.D.McMillan and Miss B.F.Stove

1980 J.R.Austin and Miss T.Austin
M.R.Edmondson and Miss D.L.Fromholtz

1981 F.D.McMillan and Miss B.F.Stove
J.R.Austin and Miss T.Austin

1982 K.Curren and Miss A.E.Smith
J.M.Lloyd and Miss W.M.Turnbull

1983 J.M.Lloyd and Miss W.M.Turnbull
S.Denton and Mrs.L.W.King

1984 J.M.Lloyd and Miss W.M.Turnbull
S.Denton and Miss K.Jordan

1985 P.McNamee and Miss M.Navratilova
J.B.Fitzgerald and Mrs.P.D.Smylie

1986 K.Flach and Miss K.Jordan
H.P.Guenthardt and Miss M.Navratilova

1987 M.J.Bates and Miss J.M.Durie
D.Cahill and Miss N.Provis

1988 S.E.Stewart and Miss Z.L.Garrison
K.Jones and Mrs.S.W.Magers

1989 J.Pugh and Miss J.Novotna
M.Kratzmann and Miss J.M.Byrne

1990 R.Leach and Miss Z.L.Garrison
J.B.Fitzgerald and Mrs.P.D.Smylie

1991 J.B.Fitzgerald and Mrs.P.D.Smylie
J.Pugh and Miss N.Zvereva

1992 C.Suk and Mrs.A.Neiland
J.Eltingh and Miss M.Oremans

1993 M.Woodforde and Miss M.Navratilova
T.Nijssen and Miss M.M.Bollegraf

1994 T.A.Woodbridge and Miss H.Sukova
T.J.Middleton and Miss L.M.McNeil

1995 J.Stark and Miss M.Navratilova
C.Suk and Miss B.C.Fernandez

1996 C.Suk and Miss H.Sukova
M.Woodforde and Mrs.A.Neiland

1997 C.Suk and Miss H.Sukova
A.Olhovskiy and Mrs.A.Neiland

1998 M.Mirnyi and Miss S.Williams
M.Bhupathi and Miss M.Lucic

1999 L.Paes and Miss L.M.Raymond
J.Bjorkman and Miss A.Kournikova

2000 D.Johnson and Miss K.Po
L.Hewitt and Miss K.Clijsters

2001 L.Friedl and Miss D.Hantuchova
M.Bryan and Mrs.A.Huber

2002 M.Bhupathi and Miss E.Likhovtseva
K.Ullyett and Miss D.Hantuchova

2003 L.Paes and Miss M.Navratilova
A.Ram and Miss A.Rodionova

2004 W.Black and Miss C.Black
T.A.Woodbridge and Miss A.Molik

2005 M.Bhupathi and Miss M.Pierce
P.Hanley and Miss T.Perebiynis

2006 A.Ram and Miss V.Zvonareva
R.Bryan and Miss V.Williams

2007 J.Murray and Miss J.Jankovic
J.Bjorkman and Miss A.Molik

2008 R.Bryan and Miss S.Stosur
M.Bryan and Miss K.Srebotnik

2009 M.Knowles and Miss A-L.Groenefeld
L.Paes and Miss C.Black

2010 L.Paes and Miss C.Black
W.Moodie and Miss L.Raymond

2011 J.Melzer and Miss I.Benesova
M.Bhupathi and Miss E.Vesnina

2012 M.Bryan and Miss L.Raymond
L.Paes and Miss E.Vesnina

2013 D.Nestor and Miss K.Mladenovic
B.Soares and Miss L.Raymond

BOYS' SINGLES

1947 K.Nielsen *S.V.Davidson*	1964 I.El Shafei *V.Korotkov*	1981 M.W.Anger *P.Cash*	1998 R.Federer *I.Labadze*
1948 S.Stockenberg *D.Vad*	1965 V.Korotkov *G.Goven*	1982 P.Cash *H.Sundstrom*	1999 J.Melzer *K.Pless*
1949 S.Stockenberg *J.A.T.Horn*	1966 V.Korotkov *B.E.Fairlie*	1983 S.Edberg *J.Frawley*	2000 N.Mahut *M.Ancic*
1950 J.A.T.Horn *K.Mobarek*	1967 M.Orantes *M.S.Estep*	1984 M.Kratzmann *S.Kruger*	2001 R.Valent *G.Muller*
1951 J.Kupferburger *K.Mobarek*	1968 J.G.Alexander *J.Thamin*	1985 L.Lavalle *E.Velez*	2002 T.Reid *L.Quahab*
1952 R.K.Wilson *T.T.Fancutt*	1969 B.Bertram *J.G.Alexander*	1986 E.Velez *J.Sanchez*	2003 F.Mergea *C.Guccione*
1953 W.A.Knight *R.Krishnan*	1970 B.Bertram *F.Gebert*	1987 D.Nargiso *J.R.Stoltenberg*	2004 G.Monfils *M.Kasiri*
1954 R.Krishnan *A.J.Cooper*	1971 R.Kreiss *S.A.Warboys*	1988 N.Pereira *G.Raoux*	2005 J.Chardy *R.Haase*
1955 M.P.Hann *J.E.Lundquist*	1972 B.Borg *C.J.Mottram*	1989 N.Kulti *T.A.Woodbridge*	2006 T.De Bakker *M.Gawron*
1956 R.Holmberg *R.G.Laver*	1973 W.Martin *C.S.Dowdeswell*	1990 L.Paes *M.Ondruska*	2007 D.Young *V.Ignatic*
1957 J.I.Tattersall *I.Ribeiro*	1974 W.Martin *Ash Amritraj*	1991 T.Enquist *M.Joyce*	2008 G.Dimitrov *H.Kontinen*
1958 E.Buchholz *P.J.Lall*	1975 C.J.Lewis *R.Ycaza*	1992 D.Skoch *B.Dunn*	2009 A.Kuznetsov *J.Cox*
1959 T.Lejus *R.W.Barnes*	1976 H.Guenthardt *P.Elter*	1993 R.Sabau *J.Szymanski*	2010 M.Fucsovics *B.Mitchell*
1960 A.R.Mandelstam *J.Mukerjea*	1977 V.A.Winitsky *T.E.Teltscher*	1994 S.Humphries *M.A.Philippoussis*	2011 L.Saville *L.Broady*
1961 C.E.Graebner *E.Blanke*	1978 I.Lendl *J.Turpin*	1995 O.Mutis *N.Kiefer*	2012 F.Peliwo *L.Saville*
1962 S.Matthews *A.Metreveli*	1979 R.Krishnan *D.Siegler*	1996 V.Voltchkov *I.Ljubicic*	2013 G.Quinzi *H.Chung*
1963 N.Kalogeropoulos *I.El Shafei*	1980 T.Tulasne *H.D.Beutel*	1997 W.Whitehouse *D.Elsner*	

BOYS' DOUBLES

1982 P.Cash and J.Frawley *R.D.Leach and J.J.Ross*	1996 D.Bracciali and J.Robichaud *D.Roberts and W.Whitehouse*	2010 L.Broady and T.Farquharson *L.Burton and G.Morgan*
1983 M.Kratzmann and S.Youl *M.Nastase and O. Rahnasto*	1997 L.Horna and N.Massu *J.Van de Westhuizen and W.Whitehouse*	2011 G.Morgan and M.Pavic *O.Golding and J.Vesely*
1984 R.Brown and R.Weiss *M.Kratzmann and J.Svensson*	1998 R.Federer and O.Rochus *M.Llodra and A.Ram*	2012 A.Harris and N.Kyrgios *M.Donati and P.Licciardi*
1985 A.Moreno and J.Yzaga *P.Korda and C.Suk*	1999 G.Coria and D.Nalbandian *T.Enev and J.Nieminem*	2013 T.Kokkinakis and N.Kyrgios *E.Couacaud and S.Napolitano*
1986 T.Carbonell and P.Korda *S.Barr and H.Karrasch*	2000 D.Coene and K.Vliegen *A.Banks and B.Riby*	
1987 J.Stoltenberg and T.Woodbridge *D.Nargiso and E.Rossi*	2001 F.Dancevic and G.Lapentti *B.Echagaray and S.Gonzales*	
1988 J.Stoltenberg and T.Woodbridge *D.Rikl and T.Zdrazila*	2002 F.Mergea and H.Tecau *B.Baker and B.Ram*	
1989 J.Palmer and J.Stark *J-L.De Jager and W.R.Ferreira*	2003 F.Mergea and H.Tecau *A.Feeney and C.Guccione*	
1990 S.Lareau and S.Leblanc *C.Marsh and M.Ondruska*	2004 B.Evans and S.Oudsema *R.Haase and V.Troicki*	
1991 K.Alami and G.Rusedski *J-L.De Jager and A.Medvedev*	2005 J.Levine and M.Shabaz *S.Groth and A.Kennaugh*	
1992 S.Baldas and S.Draper *M. S.Bhupathi and N.Kirtane*	2006 K.Damico and N.Schnugg *M.Klizan and A.Martin*	
1993 S.Downs and J.Greenhalgh *N.Godwin and G.Williams*	2007 D.Lopez and M.Trevisan *R.Jebavy and M.Klizan*	
1994 B.Ellwood and M.Philippoussis *V.Platenik and R.Schlachter*	2008 C-P.Hsieh and T-H.Yang *M.Reid and B.Tomic*	
1995 M.Lee and J.M.Trotman *A.Hernandez and M.Puerta*	2009 P-H.Herbert and K.Krawietz *J.Obry and A.Puget*	

GIRLS' SINGLES

1947 Miss G.Domken	1964 Miss P.Bartkowicz	1981 Miss Z.Garrison	1998 Miss K.Srebotnik
Miss B.Wallen	*Miss E.Subirats*	*Miss R.R.Uys*	*Miss K.Clijsters*
1948 Miss O.Miskova	1965 Miss O.Morozova	1982 Miss C.Tanvier	1999 Miss I.Tulyagnova
Miss V.Rigollet	*Miss R.Giscarfe*	*Miss H.Sukova*	*Miss L.Krasnoroutskaya*
1949 Miss C.Mercelis	1966 Miss B.Lindstrom	1983 Miss P.Paradis	2000 Miss M.E.Salerni
Miss J.S.V.Partridge	*Miss J.A.Congdon*	*Miss P.Hy*	*Miss T.Perebiynis*
1950 Miss L.Cornell	1967 Miss J.Salome	1984 Miss A.N.Croft	2001 Miss A.Widjaja
Miss A. Winter	*Miss E.M.Strandberg*	*Miss E.Reinach*	*Miss D.Safina*
1951 Miss L.Cornell	1968 Miss K.Pigeon	1985 Miss A.Holikova	2002 Miss V.Douchevina
Miss S.Lazzarino	*Miss L.E.Hunt*	*Miss J.M.Byrne*	*Miss M.Sharapova*
1952 Miss F.J.l.ten Bosch	1969 Miss K.Sawamatsu	1986 Miss N.M.Zvereva	2003 Miss K.Flipkens
Miss R.Davar	*Miss B.I.Kirk*	*Miss L.Meskhi*	*Miss A.Tchakvetadze*
1953 Miss D.Kilian	1970 Miss S.Walsh	1987 Miss N.M.Zvereva	2004 Miss K.Bondarenko
Miss V.A.Pitt	*Miss M.V.Kroshina*	*Miss J.Halard*	*Miss A.Ivanovic*
1954 Miss V.A.Pitt	1971 Miss M.V.Kroschina	1988 Miss B.Schultz	2005 Miss A.Radwanska
Miss C.Monnot	*Miss S. H.Minford*	*Miss E.Derly*	*Miss T.Paszek*
1955 Miss S.M.Armstrong	1972 Miss I.Kloss	1989 Miss A.Strnadova	2006 Miss C.Wozniacki
Miss B.de Chambure	*Miss G.L.Coles*	*Miss M.J.McGrath*	*Miss M.Rybarikova*
1956 Miss A.S.Haydon	1973 Miss A.Kiyomura	1990 Miss A.Strnadova	2007 Miss U.Radwanska
Miss I.Buding	*Miss M.Navratilova*	*Miss K.Sharpe*	*Miss M.Brengle*
1957 Miss M.Arnold	1974 Miss M.Jausovec	1991 Miss B.Rittner	2008 Miss L.Robson
Miss E.Reyes	*Miss M.Simionescu*	*Miss E.Makarova*	*Miss N.Lertcheewakarn*
1958 Miss S.M.Moore	1975 Miss N.Y.Chmyreva	1992 Miss C.Rubin	2009 Miss N.Lertcheewakarn
Miss A.Dmitrieva	*Miss R.Marsikova*	*Miss L.Courtois*	*Miss K.Mladenovic*
1959 Miss J.Cross	1976 Miss N.Y.Chmyreva	1993 Miss N.Feber	2010 Miss K.Pliskova
Miss D.Schuster	*Miss M.Kruger*	*Miss R.Grande*	*Miss S.Ishizu*
1960 Miss K.Hantze	1977 Miss L.Antonoplis	1994 Miss M.Hingis	2011 Miss A.Barty
Miss L.M Hutchings	*Miss Mareen Louie*	*Miss M-R.Jeon*	*Miss I.Khromacheva*
1961 Miss G.Baksheeva	1978 Miss T.Austin	1995 Miss A.Olsza	2012 Miss E.Bouchard
Miss K.D.Chabot	*Miss H.Mandlikova*	*Miss T.Tanasugarn*	*Miss E.Svitolina*
1962 Miss G.Baksheeva	1979 Miss M.L.Piatek	1996 Miss A.Mauresmo	2013 Miss B.Bencic
Miss E.P.Terry	*Miss A.A.Moulton*	*Miss M.L.Serna*	*Miss T.Townsend*
1963 Miss D.M.Salfati	1980 Miss D.Freeman	1997 Miss C.Black	
Miss K.Dening	*Miss S.J.Leo*	*Miss A.Rippner*	

GIRLS' DOUBLES

1982 Miss B.Herr and Miss P.Barg	1994 Miss E.De Villiers and Miss E.E.Jelfs	2005 Miss V.Azarenka and Miss A.Szavay
Miss B.S.Gerken and Miss G.A.Rush	*Miss C.M.Morariu and Miss L.Varmuzova*	*Miss M.Erakovic and Miss M.Niculescu*
1983 Miss P.Fendick and Miss P.Hy	1995 Miss C.Black and Miss A.Olsza	2006 Miss A.Kleybanova and Miss A.Pavlyuchenkova
Miss C.Anderholm and Miss H.Olsson	*Miss T.Musgrove and Miss J. Richardson*	*Miss K.Antoniychuk and Miss A.Dulgheru*
1984 Miss C.Kuhlman and Miss S.Rehe	1996 Miss O.Barabanschikova and Miss A.Mauresmo	2007 Miss A.Pavlyuchenkova and Miss U.Radwanska
Miss V.Milvidskaya and Miss L.I.Savchenko	*Miss L.Osterloh and Miss S.Reeves*	*Miss M.Doi and Miss K.Nara*
1985 Miss L.Field and Miss J.Thompson	1997 Miss C.Black and Miss I.Selyutina	2008 Miss P.Hercog and Miss J.Moore
Miss E.Reinach and Miss J.A.Richardson	*Miss M.Matevzic and Miss K.Srebotnik*	*Miss I.Holland and Miss S.Peers*
1986 Miss M.Jaggard and Miss L.O'Neill	1998 Miss E.Dyrberg and Miss J.Kostanic	2009 Miss N.Lertcheewakarn and Miss S.Peers
Miss L.Meskhi and Miss N.M.Zvereva	*Miss P.Rampre and Miss I.Tulyaganova*	*Miss K.Mladenovic and Miss S.Njiric*
1987 Miss N.Medvedeva and Miss N.M.Zvereva	1999 Miss D.Bedanova and Miss M.E.Salerni	2010 Miss T.Babos and Miss S.Stephens
Miss I.S.Kim and Miss P.M.Moreno	*Miss T.Perebiynis and Miss I.Tulyaganova*	*Miss I.Khromacheva and Miss E.Svitolina*
1988 Miss J.A.Faull and Miss R.McQuillan	2000 Miss I.Gaspar and Miss T.Perebiynis	2011 Miss E.Bouchard and Miss G.Min
Miss A.Dechaume and Miss E.Derly	*Miss D.Bedanova and Miss M.E.Salerni*	*Miss D.Schuurs and Miss Hao Chen Tang*
1989 Miss J.Capriati and Miss M.McGrath	2001 Miss G.Dulko and Miss A.Harkleroad	2012 Miss E.Bouchard and Miss T.Townsend
Miss A.Strnadova and Miss E.Sviglerova	*Miss C.Horiatopoulos and Miss B.Mattek*	*Miss B.Bencic and Miss A.Konjuh*
1990 Miss K.Habsudova and Miss A.Strnadova	2002 Miss E.Clijsters and Miss B.Strycova	2013 Miss B.Krejcikova and Miss K.Siniakova
Miss N.J.Pratt and Miss K.Sharpe	*Miss A.Baker and Miss A-L.Groenfeld*	*Miss A.Kalinina and Miss I.Shymanovich*
1991 Miss C.Barclay and Miss L.Zaltz	2003 Miss A.Kleybanova and Miss S.Mirza	
Miss J.Limmer and Miss A.Woolcock	*Miss K.Bohmova and Miss M.Krajicek*	
1992 Miss M.Avotins and Miss L.McShea	2004 Miss V.Azarenka and Miss V.Havartsova	
Miss P.Nelson and Miss J.Steven	*Miss M.Erakovic and Miss M.Niculescu*	
1993 Miss L.Courtois and Miss N.Feber		
Miss H.Mochizuki and Miss Y.Yoshida		

ROLEX
The Rolex Wimbledon Picture of the Year Competition 2013

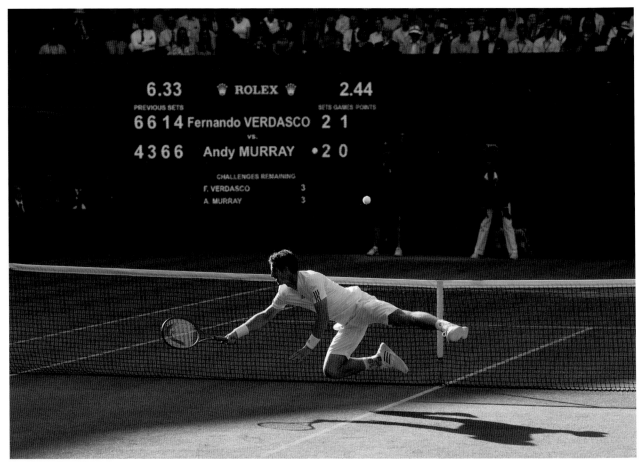

Winner
Andy Murray dives full-length to meet a volley in the fifth set of his epic quarter-final match with Fernando Verdasco

Photographer
Edward Whitaker
(*Racing Post*)

Runner-up
Novak Djokovic and Andy Murray make their way from the locker room to Centre Court before battle commences in the men's singles final

Photographer
Antoine Couvercelle
(*Tennis Magazine* France)